Conceived in Hope

The Struggles of Biblical Mothers in the Tapestry of Redemption

מגיד
MAGGID

Chana Tannenbaum

CONCEIVED IN HOPE

THE STRUGGLES OF BIBLICAL MOTHERS
IN THE TAPESTRY OF REDEMPTION

Maggid Books

Conceived in Hope
The Struggles of Biblical Mothers in the Tapestry of Redemption

First Edition, 2024

Maggid Books
An imprint of Koren Publishers Jerusalem Ltd.

POB 8531, New Milford, CT 06776-8531, USA
& POB 4044, Jerusalem 9104001, Israel
www.korenpub.com

The publication of this book was made possible
through the generous support of *The Jewish Book Trust*.

ISBN 978-1-59264-665-4, *hardcover*

A CIP catalogue record for this title is
available from the British Library

Printed and bound in the United States

Dedicated to all the women
who pray for a child and wait with hope

In loving memory of

Dr. Allen Goldstein ***z"l,***

a shining example of the seamless integration
of Torah and secular knowledge.
A genuine Torah scholar, who for decades delivered
a captivating and insightful shiur –
he also received wide acclaim as a supremely
talented physician and surgeon.

Contents

PART THREE

WOMEN WHO FIGHT FOR OR LOSE THEIR CHILDREN

PART FOUR

WOMEN WHOSE CHILDREN PLAY A ROLE IN THE SALVATION OF THE WORLD

Introduction

Even now in the twenty-first century, women are fighting for equal rights. In some places, it is about the right of women to earn the same salaries as their male colleagues. In other places, women fight for the freedom to drive a car or attend university. And in some areas of the world, women struggle for the right to fundamental liberties and fairness.

In the ancient world in general, and in the biblical world specifically, men dominated society, religion, and the home. In this highly patriarchal society, women were often abused, ignored, undervalued, and unheard. A woman's identity, value, sustenance – her very existence – were directly connected to the men she was associated with, usually her father, brother, husband, or son. A woman's ability to give birth was one of her primary responsibilities and an important factor in her social standing.

No society can have continuity without its female members, yet their contribution seems to be underappreciated. It is women who are birthing, feeding, nurturing, raising, educating, and instilling values in the future male leaders.

The biblical woman is portrayed in contradictory fashions. On the one hand, she is often a victim, unnamed, uncounted, and with questionable value. Yet we also meet women in the Bible who are leaders and prophetesses. We meet opinionated "women to watch for," and the female is commonly used as a metaphor for elements of incredible value including the Jewish nation, the Torah, and the soul.

The motif of birth and mothering, whether present or glaringly lacking, runs through many biblical stories and prophecies. The continuation of civilization in general, and of a specific nation in particular, is dependent on the birth and subsequent education of the next generations. The healthy family unit is one of the foundations of successful societal growth. It is not surprising that the relationship between God and the Jewish people is described metaphorically in terms of family. It is through our human relationships that we learn to relate to God and view Him as King, Father, and Lover.

God is commonly viewed as a male figure, such as in the verse in Malachi (2:10): "Do we not all have one Father? Were we not all created by one God?" or the phrase often repeated in prayer, *Avinu Malkeinu*, "Our Father, our King." Song of Songs describes God as the *dod*, "beloved" (male form) and the nation as the *raya*, "darling" (female form), a couple who repeatedly declare their love for one another and are constantly striving to unite.

On occasion, God is poignantly represented as a mother figure. In *Parashat Haazinu* (Deut. 32:18), Moses predicts the future, declaring that the Israelites will forget God, who "gave you birth." The mother-child bond is known to be exceedingly strong, so Moses questions how it is possible that the Israelites would reject and ignore such an innate connection to God. Other relationships, even marriage, can be severed, but the genetic connection between a parent and a child can never be denied.

Isaiah 42 is another instance where God is likened to a mother. In the text's description of God taking revenge on the enemies of His people, He cries out like a woman giving birth (42:14). The metaphor teaches us that the salvation of the people will emerge from the destruction of their enemies. The birth pangs represent the current suffering. A woman cries out in pain, but she bears the terrible discomfort knowing that it is necessary for the end result.

When the nation bemoans its fate, crying that God has abandoned it and its holy city, He answers: "Can a mother forget her own baby; can she fail to care for the child of her womb?" (Is. 49:15). Israel and Jerusalem are as dear to God as a child is to its mother. The prophecy continues, saying that even if it were possible for God to forget His children, He promises never to do so. Jerusalem will again be filled with her children (Is. 49:17–21). In order to comfort the nation that feels bereft, rejected, and despondent, the prophet uses the metaphor of a mother – symbolizing an indestructible bond – to guarantee redemption and the return to God and Jerusalem.

Isaiah continues the metaphor in comforting Jerusalem, declaring that the child will be delivered even before the labor pains begin, meaning that the redemption will be swift and painless (66:7). The children of Jerusalem will be comforted as a newborn nursing from his mother. Where is the source of this comfort? The verse does not ascribe it to anyone, but it is God all along who is comforting the people and the city. Throughout this prophecy, God is described as a mother who suckles, comforts, and cares for the child more than anyone else. The prophet chooses this metaphor because there is no relationship that comes close to the depth and meaning of a mother's love. The primary attribute of God, especially of His four-letter name, is compassion. The Hebrew word for compassion is *raḥamim*, which comes from the word *reḥem*, meaning "womb."

If This Is So, Why Am I Living?

The challenges of infertility have affected women throughout history, including a surprisingly large number of women in the Bible. This timeless struggle still resonates today in the role of women in the Jewish family, society, and nation.

Biblical women contended with their place in a male-dominated society. For the vast majority, their role was centered on their ability to have children. But what happened to the woman who was barren, or the woman who lost her children? How did this affect her position and relationship to the world around her, including men, society in general, and God? What happened when some barren women did eventually give birth? How did the role of motherhood, as opposed to the unique role of a woman as an individual, manifest itself? What is the lesson these seemingly secondary characters add to our understanding of the role of biblical women?

Females who struggle in the Bible can be divided into four categories:

1. Barren women who eventually bear children
   a. The matriarchs Sarah, Rebecca, Rachel, and Leah
   b. Hazlelponi (wife of Manoah, mother of Samson)
   c. Hannah
   d. The Shunamite woman
2. Barren women who never bear children
   a. Daughter of Jephthah
   b. Batya
   c. Michal
   d. Tamar, daughter of David
3. Women who fight for or lose their children
   a. Judgment of Solomon
   b. The wife of Obadiah
   c. Rizpah
   d. Athaliah
4. Women whose children play a role in the salvation of the world
   a. Daughters of Lot
   b. Tamar, daughter-in-law of Judah
   c. Ruth
   d. Jerusalem

We begin by exploring the stories of women who, although they were initially barren, do eventually bear children. We look at why they were barren, and how they react to their difficulties and the eventual arrival of their offspring.

The second group of women is comprised of those who never get to experience motherhood, mostly due to their victimization by men. The lack of children, and of continuation, is often tragic, but not necessarily so.

In the third group are women who have children, fight for them, and ultimately lose them. Is it better to have loved and lost than not to have loved at all?

Last, as we explore the children who become part of the salvation of the world, we learn that humanity's ultimate redemption has been established through a man born under questionable circumstances.

Acknowledgments

מָה־אָשִׁיב לַה׳ כׇּל־תַּגְמוּלוֹהִי עָלָי (תהלים קטז:יב)

How can I repay the L*ORD*
for all His bounties to me? (Ps. 116:12)

It is evident that without the grace of God, none of us could endure even for a moment. Our lives are a divine gift, and in gratitude, we owe Him our deepest thanks and adoration. This book serves as a testament to the countless blessings bestowed upon me by God. My hope is that this work fulfills its purpose and honors His name, while I pray for the continued opportunity to teach and share His word for many years to come.

The genesis of documenting my classes originated from the unsettling event known as the "kidnapping of the boys," among whom was our neighbor, Naftali Frankel *Hy"d*. During those difficult days, I asked myself, "In my distress I called on the Lord; the Lord answered me and set me free (Ps. 118:5)."

As I write this page, three of my sons are currently summoned to defend our fundamental right to inhabit this world. It has indeed been over eight years since the inception of this book, transitioning it from a mere idea to a tangible reality. The process of writing has served as a beacon, guiding me toward a place of solace and reassurance, allowing me to reestablish a profound connection to our source.

Without the unwavering support, encouragement, and assistance of numerous individuals, this endeavor would have remained but a distant aspiration.

My parents, Dr. Allen Goldstein, *z"l*, and my mother, Shulamith Goldstein, were the bedrock of my passion for learning and my unwavering pursuit of a deeper understanding of Torah. They fostered an environment where Torah infused every aspect of our daily lives, not just as a subject of study, but as a guiding principle that we lived and breathed. Their steadfast support and encouragement propelled me forward, celebrating my achievements and inspiring me to reach for further goals.

It is through years of teaching, or rather, through the rich interactions and engagements with my students, that I have gained new perspectives, attitudes, and insights. I am profoundly grateful to all those who have studied alongside me over the years, for they have played an instrumental role in shaping me into the educator I have become.

A heartfelt thank you is owed to the women who courageously opened their hearts, allowing the public a glimpse into their poignant memories: Leah, Sherri, Anna, and Anne. Special recognition is also due to Anne, whose instrumental efforts were pivotal in bringing this book to fruition.

My thanks to Yael Nuewirt, who graciously allowed her wonderful painting to appear on the cover of my book. I am also grateful to an anonymous sponsor who supported the publication of this book and enabled it to come to fruition.

I extend my sincere thanks to the entire team at Koren Publishers: Matthew Miller, Reuven Ziegler, Caryn Meltz, Aryeh Grossman, Alex Drucker, Rina Ben Gal, Kate Gerstler, Tali Simon, and Debbie Ismailoff, all of whom have contributed to transforming this book from a rough draft into a polished gem. Your dedication and expertise have turned what was once a mere clod of earth into a precious stone.

To my husband, Moshe, your patience, feedback, and support are woven into every aspect of this book. It would never have taken flight without you by my side. And to my children, their spouses, and their children, who continually inspire me with their achievements and successes, I am immensely proud of the remarkable adults you have grown into.

Part One

Barren Women Who Eventually Bear Children

הנך הרה וילדת בן

(Genesis 16:11)

Chapter 1

Barren Matriarchs

In mythology and folklore throughout the world, the conception and birth of the hero is often extraordinary. Death and misfortune are common themes in the tragic tales of infertile women, including the epic poem originating in ancient Madagascar that begins with a barren woman giving birth to the hero Ibonia; the hero of Irish mythology, Conall Cearnach, born to the barren Findchoem, who becomes pregnant after drinking well water that contains a worm;[1] and Lamia of ancient Greek mythology, whose barrenness is a punishment inflicted by the jealous Hera, wife of Zeus (since Hera cannot bear her own children, she attacks and kills the children of others).[2]

There is a talmudic saying that a barren person is like one who is dead (Avoda Zara 5a). Barrenness is an affliction that worsens with the passage of time, because as one ages it becomes harder to conceive. The

1. Anna June Pagé, "Birth Narratives in Indo-European Mythology" (PhD diss., University of California, Los Angeles, 2014). Available at: https://escholarship.org/content/qt71m1f09s/qt71m1f09s_noSplash_f6ccebb2e4216e2f08eb6cd1410c1bbf.pdf.
2. Linda McGuire, "From Greek Myth to Medieval Witches: Infertile Women as Monstrous and Evil." Available at: https://docplayer.net/29530550-From-greek-myth-to-medieval-witches-infertile-women-as-monstrous-and-evil-linda-mcguire.html.

emotional pain also increases over time, as the infertile couple watches other families grow while they remain stuck. With no children to carry on their name, ideals, and legacy, an infertile couple's future often feels empty, perhaps even worthless. They may feel that their lives are but a blip in history, as little will remain once they are gone. The Hebrew word for barren is *akar,* derived from the root meaning "to pluck" or "to uproot," the very opposite of "to plant," indicating a lack of hope for growth, blossoming, or continuation – only certain death.

Sarah, Rebecca, Rachel, and Leah, the mothers of the Jewish people, are all considered barren women.[3] God brought the world into existence out of His desire to create a world with purpose and meaning.[4] He created Adam and Eve with a goal: after blessing all of creation, God commands them to "be fertile and multiply." Eve's name in Hebrew is Ḥava – which means "mother of all life" – because God bestowed on her the unique ability to create another living being within her body. There, in a completely safe environment, the fetus develops, grows, and is nourished until it becomes a viable human being.

Eve also has a "counter-name": *Isha,* which complements Adam's role of *ish,* man. According to Rabbi Isaac Arama, the names Ḥava and Isha represent two different functions of womankind.[5] In her role as *Isha,* woman, she was brought into this world to work alongside man in making it a better place through intelligence and morality. As Ḥava, she fulfills the role of the mother. Although a barren woman may not be able to fulfill the role of Ḥava, she can succeed brilliantly in the role of Isha.

Still, one wonders: Why do all of the matriarchs suffer this same challenge? In the ancient Near East, having children was a significant desire for women, defining their status and worth. Barrenness was (and still is) considered an unnatural state. In order to have continuity and achieve God's purpose, the world needs to be fertile in all respects: produce, animals, and humans. Birth is not only a personal experience; it is significant to the continued existence of society as a whole. Most healthy couples are able to procreate; those who are unable to conceive are in

3. *Pesikta DeRav Kahana* 20.
4. Rashi on Genesis 1:1.
5. *Akedat Yitzḥak* on Genesis 9:1–7.

the minority. When a barren couple has a child, they join the quotidian, finally feeling that they are just like everyone else.

For a couple struggling with infertility, the birth of a child is keenly felt to be nothing short of miraculous. God does not perform miracles by suspending the natural order of events flippantly. Miracles do not just "happen." According to the Gemara, God bestows on mankind many different abilities in this world – planting, harvesting, baking, sewing. These are all forms of creation that are well within man's capabilities. However, there are three "keys" that God Himself maintains: the keys to birth, resurrection, and rain (Taanit 2a). These three life-giving experiences are miraculous and should be viewed as such.

Prayer

The Gemara questions why our matriarchs were barren and answers that it is "because He desires the prayers of the righteous" (Yevamot 64a). God asks: "If My people are wealthy, beautiful, and smart, why do they need Me?"[6] This answer is even more difficult to understand than the question! God has no desires or needs, so how are we to understand this answer, which seemingly attributes to God the simple mortal longing to feel needed?

Prayer has the ability to bend the rules of nature. With prayer, even those who are barren can have children, against all odds. The Gemara maintains that not only was Sarah barren, but she actually lacked a uterus.[7] It is hard to imagine slimmer odds than those.

Man's fundamental purpose in this world is to recognize God and glorify His name. Prayer is the ultimate expression of this goal. Through his supplication, man increases the manifestation of God's presence in this world. This is what it meant by the statement that God "desires" prayer: through the supplicant's sincere prayer, God's immanence is affirmed and magnified.[8] Sincere prayer is based on man's intense recognition of his dependence on God, the absolute realization that all that we

6. *Tanḥuma, Toldot* 9.
7. Yevamot 64a.
8. Rabbeinu Bahya on Genesis 25:21.

have is but a gift from God. Without God's beneficence man would not even exist, let alone flourish. Even the most basic of functions that the world takes for granted, such as waking in the morning, and the body's natural processes – including pregnancy and birth – happen because God has willed it to be so.

The lesson we learn from the matriarchs' struggles with fertility is about the relationship one develops with God through prayer, as well as the power that prayer has to change negative decrees. God listens and responds, though perhaps not always in the way we desire. Prayer helps us to accept God's decree and gives us strength to cope.

Barren women are sometimes the loneliest people on earth. On the topic of loneliness, Rabbi Joseph B. Soloveitchik describes the pain and the necessary dependence on God: "I despair because I am lonely and, hence, feel frustrated. On the other hand, I also feel invigorated because this very experience of loneliness presses everything in me into the service of God."[9]

Serving God

Although we have seen that the Gemara's lesson from infertility is the importance of prayer, the biblical text only mentions the prayers of one matriarch: Rebecca. And even then, the reference is indirect: The verse (Gen. 25:21) says that Rebecca's husband prayed *lenokhaḥ*, sometimes translated as "opposite her," suggesting that perhaps she prayed with him.[10] If the message of infertility was prayer alone, we would expect to see many lengthy prayers like those of Hannah included in the text of the Tanakh.[11]

The Midrash offers several rather difficult explanations for the infertility of our forebears.[12] One suggestion is that God wanted these women to spend the years of their prime unencumbered by the time

---

9. Rabbi Joseph B. Soloveitchik, "The Lonely Man of Faith," *Tradition* (Summer 1965): 7.
10. See Rashi there. He explains that Isaac and Rebecca stood in opposite corners of the room while praying to God for a child.
11. See the chapter on Hannah in this volume.
12. Song of Songs Rabba 2.

and emotional constraints of child-rearing so that they would be fully available to spread His word.[13] Only in their old age, after giving meaning and purpose to the lives of others, were they free to have children of their own.[14] Just as the previous explanation presented prayer as the way to bring recognition of God into the soul of the petitioner, here barrenness is presented as the very thing that enabled the matriarchs to inspire the souls of others. The biblical text says that when Abraham left his birthplace at the command of God, he took with him *hanefesh asher asu,* literally, "the souls they made" (Gen. 12:5). Rashi explains that he and Sarah "made" souls by teaching people Torah: Abraham taught the men and Sarah taught the women. We could also suggest that Rebecca was occupied with teaching, based on the Rashi that says that she experienced terrible pains when she passed places of idol worship.[15] Why didn't she just avoid those places? The explanation is that she was engaged in spreading belief in God.

Later in Genesis, we learn of Rachel stealing her father's idols (31:30–34), but it is unclear as to whether her purpose was educational. In fact, none of these sources paint a clear picture of the matriarchs actually being engaged in teaching others about God.

Beauty

Another opinion is that God caused the matriarchs to be barren so they could maintain their beauty and attractiveness for their husbands.[16] A strong bond between husband and wife is essential for establishing a Jewish home, and that secure spousal relationship is the foundation for a stable family, and on a larger scale, for building a nation. The beauty of the matriarchs is clearly stated in the text: Sarah's beauty is recognized by Abraham, and it brings trouble in Egypt (Gen. 12:11–20). Rebecca is described as beautiful when the servant Eliezer meets her (24:16), and again at least twenty years later in Gerar (26:7). Rachel is also identified

13. See Rashi on Genesis 12:5.
14. Rabbi Zalman Sorotzkin, *Oznayim LaTorah* on Genesis 11:30.
15. Rashi on Genesis 25:22.
16. Song of Songs Rabba 2:8.

as beautiful (29:17), and Leah is described as "soft-eyed," which Rashbam says indicates beauty as well.[17]

National Benefit

In a different vein, the Midrash says that by postponing the birth of Isaac, God was able to shorten the Egyptian exile. Rabbeinu Bahya explains that since God calculated the Egyptian bondage from the time of the *Brit Bein HaBetarim*, God's covenant with Abraham, the more time that elapsed before the actual birth of the forefathers Isaac and Jacob, the fewer years of servitude would remain.[18] These suggestions teach us that all pain and suffering has value as part of a much broader divine picture that we are unable to perceive. The suffering endured by an individual may have a long-term benefit that is not readily apparent to the sufferer.

Summary

The Midrash proffers these answers in an effort to identify a purpose, or perhaps even an advantage, to experiencing infertility. It is a basic tenet of Judaism that everything comes from God and therefore has a purpose. The Midrash also provides different approaches for coping with human suffering, such as prayer, investment in other activities, finding support from others, and developing a broader vision and perspective.[19] The matriarchs took decisive action instead of allowing themselves to remain entangled in their pain. These actions included prayer, providing their husbands with a second wife, or turning their pain into a growth experience for themselves or a way to improve their environment.

The barrenness suffered by the foremothers allowed space for them to develop associations with those around them, in particular with God, since it was to Him they prayed and through Him that their

17. Rashbam on Genesis 29:17.
18. See Rabbeinu Bahya on Genesis 25:21. This idea is also found in Genesis Rabba, *Lekh Lekha* 45:4.
19. Heard from Ariel Tuchfeld.

prayers were answered. They were able to influence their spouses and help them make correct decisions. Lastly, they were able to relate to others around them, educating, hosting, teaching, and helping fill the world with the knowledge of God.

Still, none of these answers are satisfying. After all, the main goal of the foremothers is the formation of the nation of Israel. Rabbi Abraham Isaac Kook suggests that their barrenness gave them a complete break from their biological past.[20] The fact that the birth of their children is miraculous teaches us that they were not just a continuation of previous generations, but rather a completely new beginning. This is why Abraham and Isaac were also considered to be barren.

The children of Israel are viewed as God's children (Deut. 14:1). Their birth as a nation was miraculous, as is their continued existence. There is no other way to explain how they have not been destroyed by the numerous pogroms, exiles, and massacres throughout the generations. A tale is told of Fredrick the Great of Prussia, who asked his philosophers for proof of God's existence. The answer he received was: "The Jews, sire, the Jews."

The matriarchs all had to contend with different forms of barrenness preventing the blossoming of future potential. This lack of biological children is also reflected in the infertility of the Land of Israel. The land also represents potential. Mother Earth should be the womb developing the produce that we need to exist. Although promised to the forefathers, the Land of Israel was found to be unfruitful, suffering periods of infertility within fertility, with famines in the times of Abraham, Isaac, and Jacob. Miracles brought about the birth of the Jewish nation, as well as the burgeoning of the Land of Israel. As gifts from God, children and the Land of Israel each serve a special purpose in this world, and the existence of both is miraculous.[21] Each has its own set of rules and its own relationship to God.

Repentance, also a miraculous gift from God, obligates us to continue to give birth to ourselves over and over again, to fulfill the

20. *Tallelei Orot* 267.

21. Heard from Rabbi Chaim Sabato.

responsibility that comes with being God's children, returning to our Creator and recreating our bond with Him.

SARAH

From the very first time we are introduced to Sarah, the Torah identifies her as barren (Gen. 11:30). The subject of her lack of descendants runs through many of the coming stories. Sarah's inability to conceive is described after a long list of verses depicting the generations between Noah and Abraham, with everything proceeding according to nature until the pattern stops with Sarah. She is unable to extend the generations; she cannot continue the Creation story. This seems to be an important part of her identity, as it is the only fact mentioned. The Sages point out that the double terminology used in Genesis 11:30 describing Sarah as both barren and having no offspring indicates that she did not even have a uterus (Yevamot 64a). One wonders if this was a fact known to Sarah in the time before X-rays and ultrasounds. Did she go into the marriage knowing that she couldn't have children? Was Abraham aware of this?

In the preceding verse (Gen. 11:29), Sarah is referred to as Yiskah.[22] This name reflects Sarah's spiritual prowess, physical beauty, and leadership skills, while the name Sarah connotes nobility. Yet with all these myriad talents she is unable to have children. The future mother of the entire nation can't naturally bring children into this world.

In God's first communication with Abraham, He promises to make him into a great nation when he leaves his birthplace, his father's home, and journeys to the land that God will show him. God also promises that the land will be inherited by Abraham's children (Gen. 12:7). In an act of true faith, Abraham believes what God tells him. Sarah, who did not benefit from hearing the command directly from God, packs their bags without question.

Once Abraham, Sarah, and their entourage arrive in Canaan, a famine plagues the land, and they are forced to relocate to Egypt.[23] In

22. Rashi on Genesis 11:29.

23. The Sages are divided on how to view this descent. Rashi says they were correct in

an effort to save Abraham's life (Abraham fears that an Egyptian will kill him in order to take Sarah), the couple insists that they are brother and sister. Does Abraham identify their relationship this way because it has not produced offspring?

Sarah is promptly abducted to Pharaoh's palace as a result of her exceptional beauty, and gifts are given to her "brother." Pharaoh and his household are then smitten with plagues *al devar Sarai*, which Rashi explains as "on account of Sarai" (Gen. 12:17). According to the Midrash, this phrase means "according to the words of Sarai," as Sarah prayed to God: "I followed Abraham based totally on faith, and this is my reward?"[24] Although in the text, Sarah is silent, a seemingly passive victim, the Midrash describes her influencing and affecting her destiny through prayer. Another opinion in the Midrash suggests that the plagues that afflicted Pharaoh were actually based on Sarah's words, meaning that she was the one who brought down God's wrath on the Egyptians.[25] The fact that Sarah is saved and returned to Abraham is an indication that God chooses Sarah, just as He chose Abraham, despite – or maybe because of – her barrenness.[26]

After ten years of living in the Land of Israel,[27] it seems that Sarah despairs of having biological children. She willingly introduces a competitor into her home by encouraging her husband to marry her maidservant, Hagar.[28] Sarah hopes that from this union, a son will be born, and through him, she will "build a family" (Gen. 16:2). Sarah clearly states her belief that a woman's ability to procreate lies in the hands of God (16:2). According to Rashi, Sarah actually hopes that because of this

relocating, while Nahmanides considers it a sin.

24. Genesis Rabba 41:2.

25. Ibid.

26. Y. Grossman, *Abraham: A Story of a Journey* [Hebrew] (Rishon LeZion: Yedioth Books, 2014), 57.

27. Genesis Rabba 45:3 explains that it was only after being in the Land of Israel for ten years that Sarah considered taking action, based on the halakha that a woman is considered barren after ten years of childlessness. The many years that she spent outside of Israel are not included in the count.

28. According to Genesis Rabba 45:1, Hagar is the daughter of Pharaoh. Recognizing Sarah's greatness, Pharaoh decided that his daughter would be better off as a slave in Sarah's home than a princess in his.

selfless move, she will be rewarded with her own offspring,[29] while Radak assumes that Sarah would raise the child born to Hagar and Abraham as her own, filling her house with noise and joy.[30]

Nahmanides points out that although Abraham strongly desired children, he would not have made this move without explicit permission and encouragement from Sarah.[31] In the preceding chapter, Abraham cries out to God, "What will You have given me if I remain childless?" (Gen. 15:2). God promises him a biological child, with descendants that will ultimately outnumber the stars – but not necessarily with Sarah. This could explain why Sarah accuses Abraham, saying, "The abuse I suffer is your fault" (Gen. 16:5). Perhaps she is saying that he should have asked God for the child to be from her.

Unwilling to accept her current situation, Sarah solves her intense desire for motherhood in the only way she can think of doing. According to Mesopotamian law, a barren wife could present her husband with a slave and acknowledge their children as her own. Hagar and Abraham indeed go on to have a son, Ishmael, whose birth is not described as bringing any joy or even acknowledgment of a promise fulfilled by God. Hagar's pregnancy and subsequent lack of respect for Sarah (Gen. 16:4) cause tension in the household. Telling the story from Hagar's perspective, the verse says that Sarah treated Hagar harshly, and so she flees (Gen. 16:6). However, an angel of God tells her to return. Nahmanides[32] and Radak view Sarah's behavior and Abraham's silent acquiescence as a sin, resulting in the future punishment of their children under the sword of Hagar's son Ishmael. Tosefta disagrees, proposing that all of Sarah's actions stem from her prophetic abilities and are thus sanctioned by God.[33] The Netziv also disagrees with Nahmanides and Radak. He says that the persecution of Hagar was justified, and that not only was Sarah defending her own honor, she was defending the honor of God as well.[34]

---

29. Rashi on Genesis 16:2.
30. Radak on Genesis 16:2.
31. Nahmanides on Genesis 16:2.
32. Nahmanides on Genesis 16:6.
33. Tosefta on Y. Sota 5:7.
34. *Harḥev Davar* 15:6.

In the next chapter, Abraham is given the commandment of circumcision. During this event, God changes the names of Abraham and Sarah from the original versions, Avram and Sarai, and promises that Sarah will bear a son. It is surprising that Sarah is included in the experience surrounding the circumcision, as it is seemingly an event exclusive to the male members of the household. For both Abraham and Sarah, the name change indicates a change of status – they are about to become parents – and they both respond with *tzeḥok,* laughter. Although the Torah uses the word *tzeḥok* to describe the reactions of both Abraham and Sarah, Onkelos notes God's negative reaction to Sarah's laughter and translates the word differently in the two instances. Abraham's laughter is translated as a joyful one,[35] whereas Sarah's is cynical. He explains that when Sarah overheard the angel delivering the message about the future birth of Isaac, she laughed cynically at the preposterousness of the idea.[36]

Yet Sarah does have the child as promised by God, when He "remembered her" (Gen. 21:1). This birth brings with it the joy and gladness that accompanies a miracle (Gen. 20:7). The child's God-given name, Isaac, contains within it an element of *tzeḥok.* According to Rabbi Samson Raphael Hirsch, this verb describes anything that strikes us as unexpected, or even absurd.[37] For a man of one hundred to have a child with his ninety-year-old wife does indeed seem unbelievable and absurd. God waited until they were at ages when it seemed impossible to have a child, and then He gave them one. Abraham and Sarah's personal miracle symbolizes the unnatural and incredible existence of the entire Jewish nation. From its inception and throughout history, the survival of the Jewish people has defied natural events. As a people, we identify with *tzeḥok.*

35. Onkelos on Genesis 17:17.
36. Onkelos on Genesis 18:12.
37. Rabbi Samson Raphael Hirsch on Genesis 17:17.

The difference between the reactions of Abraham and Sarah, and the difference in their laughter, is also due to the source of the information. Abraham heard directly from God that he would have a child with Sarah. When he received the news, he was occupied with the circumcision and did not immediately go to share the message with her. When the angels came to Sarah's tent, she perceived them as regular travelers and thought they were simply giving her an unlikely blessing – especially because it seemed clear that there was no chance of it being fulfilled.[38] It is easy to understand Sarah's hesitation and her unwillingness to believe that such a thing could happen, yet we know that God can do anything, and so understandable though her reaction may be, she is still faulted for it.[39]

Perhaps Abraham bore some of the guilt for Sarah's cynical laughter, prompting God to include him in the reprimand. Abraham questions Sarah about the laughter, which she promptly denies. Sarah could have shared her view with him, explaining that it was simply impossible and beyond human nature for them to have a son. In affirming her laughter (Gen. 18:15), Abraham gives Sarah the tools to concede to the implausible, opening her to the miracle of conception.[40] His acknowledgment opens the door to the impossible.

The next chapter, Genesis 20, describes Sarah being taken to the house of Abimelech, king of Gerar. At first glance, the reader's sympathies lie with the king, who claims innocence and pure intentions. Surprisingly, we discover that God plagues Abimelech's household with a form of barrenness, in which the wombs of the whole household are shut. Abraham prays for their complete recovery and through his prayers, Sarah is also cured from her barrenness.

Sarah becomes pregnant and delivers a son (Gen. 21:2). With the birth of Isaac, we hear about the emotional pain that Sarah suffered, as she declares, "God has brought me laughter; all those who hear will laugh with me" (Gen. 21:6). Before the birth of Isaac, Sarah was an outcast

---

38. See Sforno on Genesis 18:12 and Nahmanides on Genesis 18:15.
39. The commentators disagree about whether it was God or Abraham who spoke to Sarah.
40. Grossman, *Abraham*, 173.

in society. She felt that she was a failure to her husband because she could not bear his children. Her statement here emphasizes the supernatural quality of Isaac's birth, and it also indicates repentance for her cynical laughter earlier. Sarah uses the word *tzeḥok* twice, this time to denote her sincere happiness and joy at the totally unexpected blessing coming to fruition.

Later, while celebrating the weaning of Isaac, Sarah discovers Ishmael behaving inappropriately in Abraham's house. She demands that Abraham remove the negative influence from the house, lest Ishmael induce Isaac to also act in an unbecoming manner. Sara witnessed Ishmael "mocking." At face value, this might suggest Ishmael was quarreling over inheritance. However, according to Rashi, this action alludes to the three cardinal sins of adultery, murder, and idol worship. It is here that we see Sarah as a responsible, determined mother of her biological son and all future generations. Sarah sees and understands, as is confirmed by God, that Ishmael cannot coexist with Isaac in Abraham's household.

We find Sarah to be an equal partner with Abraham, as well as a prophetess on a higher level than her husband. She is the one who understands what is important for the continuation of the miraculous nation that she is birthing. The prophet Isaiah states (51:1–2): "You who chase righteousness, listen to Me, you who seek the Lord: Look to the rock you are hewed from, the quarry from which you were carved; look to your father, Abraham, to Sarah who gave you birth, for I called him, one alone, and blessed him, made him many." Isaiah defines Sarah's contribution as being the source of the wondrous nation of Israel.

Her contribution is also inextricably linked with that of her husband. It is well known that Abraham's defining character trait is kindness. The Bible shows us many examples, including the way he opens his home to guests and prays on their behalf, and the story of Abraham going to war to save his nephew, to name but a few. But without boundaries, kindness can become perverted, as seen with Lot.[41] The boundaries of Abraham's kindness are reined in by Sarah's defining character

41. Lot offers his daughters to the wild crowd in order to save his guests (demonstrating kindness without boundaries), and then his daughters rape him in order to prevent human extinction – also kindness of a sort, but certainly perverted.

trait: strength. She has the strength to tell Abraham that Ishmael and Hagar must go. Sarah and Abraham balance each other, and together they strive for perfection.

REBECCA

We meet Rebecca in Genesis 24, when she passes the test for kindness that is set up by Abraham's servant Eliezer. The servant convinces Rebecca's family to allow her to return to Canaan with him in order to marry Isaac. As Rebecca and Eliezer approach, she spots Isaac from afar, before he sees her. This idea of Rebecca seeing (or understanding) something before Isaac is a pattern that will repeat itself throughout their life together.

When she sees Isaac for the first time, Rebecca immediately falls off her camel and covers her face with a scarf. This reaction demonstrates the unique relationship that Isaac and Rebecca had, one based on awe and perhaps also fear.[42] The Torah records only one conversation between Rebecca and Isaac, unlike the many exchanges between other biblical couples that are detailed in the text. Yet the Torah also makes a point of stressing that Isaac loved Rebecca (Gen. 24:67).

The verses that follow describe the generations (Gen. 25:12–18), beginning with those of Abraham, then Ishmael, and finally Isaac, but here we come to an abrupt stop because Rebecca is barren (Gen. 25:21). The Gemara suggests that since the verse states that Isaac prayed *lenokhaḥ ishto* – which some translate as "opposite his wife" – this means that he too was infertile, and so a second wife would not have solved the problem (Yevamot 64a). According to another interpretation, the term *lenokhaḥ* indicates that Rebecca also prayed: Isaac prayed in one corner of the room, while she prayed opposite him in the other corner.[43] This approach shows Rebecca as the only foremother who prayed for a child (see above, "Serving God"). The Midrash indicates that she and Isaac prayed incessantly for years without despairing.

42. Netziv on Genesis 24:64–65.
43. Genesis Rabba 63:65, as quoted by Rashi.

Isaac is forty years old when he marries Rebecca (Gen. 25:20) and sixty (Gen. 25:26) when his sons are born. What transpired during those twenty years? Were he and Rebecca constantly praying? Did they consider the maidservant option, or perhaps adoption?[44] The text tells us nothing about those long, painful years, and it is not clear how Rebecca reacted to being barren. Should her story be lumped together with those of Sarah and Rachel?

As Rebecca is leaving her father's home, she is blessed, "Our sister, may you grow into thousands" (Gen. 24:60). The fact that it takes twenty years for Rebecca to bear children suggests that her family's blessing had no influence.[45] Though Rebecca comes from a questionable background – her father and brother are not upright individuals – thanks to her righteousness and fine character, she is given the privilege of continuing Sarah's legacy.

Instead of bringing in a second wife, Isaac prays on their behalf and Rebecca becomes pregnant. Her pregnancy is a difficult one. She questions her desire to have children, and she seeks an answer from God. While we don't know what Rebecca felt during those painful barren years, we do read of the pain she experiences during the pregnancy, which causes her deep anguish (Gen. 25:22).

The difficulty with Rebecca's pregnancy is described as children struggling within her. The source of this struggle is attributed to different causes. R. Yoḥanan proposes that the fetuses were literally trying to kill each other. Reish Lakish sees the struggle as a spiritual one, each trying to deprive the other of mitzvot. R. Berakhya asserts that the struggle in the womb shows that the differences between Esau and Jacob are predetermined and are not rational or based on actions.[46] Rashi quotes the Midrash's explanation that Rebecca does not know that she is having twins and therefore does not understand why the same child kicks when she passes a house of God and when she passes a place of idol worship (Gen. 25:22).

44. Little is known about adoption in biblical times, but the Midrash does mention cases of people taking foundlings into their homes.

45. Genesis Rabba 60:13.

46. Ibid. 63:6.

The struggle causes Rebecca to cry, "If this is so, why am I living?" (Gen. 25:22). How can we understand this phrase? Rashi suggests that Rebecca is questioning why she ever desired to become pregnant. Nahmanides rejects this explanation without explaining why, but perhaps he understands that an infertile woman would willingly accept all forms of pain and suffering in order to deliver a healthy child. Nahmanides also quotes Ibn Ezra, who says that Rebecca consulted other women and determined that her pregnancy was unusual. While she does not regret her desire to conceive, she is concerned about the fact that her pregnancy is unusual. Nahmanides rejects Ibn Ezra's idea and suggests that Rebecca is questioning her very essence and purpose in the world.[47] Sforno takes another approach entirely, proposing that Rebecca is afraid that the child will die and that she is in danger of dying in childbirth.[48]

Whatever she meant with this cry, Rebecca's response to her pain and confusion is to seek out God (Gen. 25:22). How would she do that? She may have sought out the "rabbinic" leaders of the time, Shem and Ever,[49] or she may have consulted Abraham,[50] or perhaps she herself prayed.[51] Why does she not turn to Isaac? Maybe she is embarrassed to complain about this pregnancy for which they have prayed and waited for twenty years.

Rebecca receives a prophecy explaining the battle inside her. God tells her that there are two nations in her womb, and that one nation will be stronger than the other, with the younger serving the older. It seems that she does not share this prophecy with Isaac. Since she did not turn to him with her worries previously, maybe she also lacks the ability to communicate with him now that she has received an answer. Or perhaps she wanted the twins to have an equal upbringing, and she is concerned that Isaac may become prejudiced and favor one over the other if he hears the prophecy. Alternatively, Nahmanides points out that one does not share a prophecy with a prophet.[52] Either way, just

47. Nahmanides on Genesis 25:22.
48. Sforno on Genesis 25:22.
49. Rashi on Genesis 25:22.
50. Ibn Ezra on Genesis 25:22.
51. Nahmanides on Genesis 25:22.
52. Nahmanides on Genesis 27:4.

as Abraham did not share his prophecy with Sarah, Rebecca does not share hers with Isaac.

Though Rebecca may have hoped that her sons would be treated equally by their parents, the Torah tells us that Rebecca loves Jacob absolutely, and Isaac loves Esau because he has a taste for wild game (Gen. 25:28). This dynamic, as well as the one between Rebecca and Isaac, results in the story of the stolen blessings. Rebecca overhears Isaac telling Esau that he is planning to bless him. She tells Jacob to cover himself with goat hair in order to pretend to be his brother, deceive his blind father, and appropriate the blessings for himself.

Rabbi Hirsch explains that Rebecca's goal is not to steal the blessing for Jacob but rather to demonstrate to Isaac how easily he can be tricked. She fully expects to be caught.[53] Rabbi Soloveitchik continues the point, explaining that Isaac and Rebecca disagreed about who should be the last forefather. Isaac feels that a strong person who is familiar with arms and hunting should be the ancestor of the nation. Would it be so terrible to have a little strength in the genetic makeup? Rebecca, who grew up among people like Esau, knows that this is not a prudent plan, but she cannot convince Isaac. With the deception, Rebecca shows Isaac that if necessary, Jacob is able to take on attributes of Esau, but an Esau could never become a Jacob. Isaac understands the message and blesses Jacob.[54]

We see here that it is Rebecca who decides which son will ultimately serve as the continuation of the nation after a miraculous birth. On her own initiative, she boldly intervenes to ensure the right succession of the covenant. She makes a decision that changes the course of Jewish history and the Jewish religion for good.

Isaac's defining character trait is strength, demonstrated via self-control in his willingness to give his life for God at the binding of Isaac.[55] Too much strength can have serious consequences, as it can lead to being too demanding of others and not having compassion for

53. Rabbi Samson Raphael Hirsch on Genesis 27:1.
54. Heard from Dr. Allen Goldstein, a dedicated student of the Rav.
55. This idea is based on the teaching in *Pirkei Avot* (4:1): "Who is strong? Someone who controls their inclinations."

their struggles. An excess of strength can also lead to abuse. But Isaac's strength is balanced by Rebecca, who demonstrates kindness from the outset when she offers water to both Abraham's servant and his camels. The two balance each other, and together they work toward perfection.

The Isaac/Rebecca dynamic echoes the Abraham/Sarah dynamic. Abraham's kindness is reined in by Sarah's strength, and Isaac's strength is balanced by Rebecca's kindness.

LEAH

One might be surprised to find Leah on the list of barren women, given that she births 50 percent of Jacob's children. However, the verse says that "He opened her womb" (Gen. 29:31), indicating that it was previously closed and that God's intervention was necessary to help her conceive.

The beginning of that verse discloses that God intervenes because Leah is hated. The Gemara explains that this hatred can't possibly be referring to how Jacob feels about Leah, because in such a case, it would be forbidden for them to remain married. Rather, the hatred is Leah's attitude toward Esau (Bava Batra 123a). When God sees how much Leah desires to be part of the establishment of the Jewish nation, He opens her womb.

Sforno says the hatred stems from Jacob's prophetic ability to recognize Leah's barrenness; at their first meeting, he saw in her the signs of a woman who cannot conceive.[56] Perhaps this explains why she was willing to marry him under false pretenses – it was her only hope of marriage at all.

The Midrash understands the hatred as indeed being Jacob's feeling toward Leah, and it offers several reasons, including: (1) the fact that Leah was originally destined to marry Esau, and (2) her monumental deception of Jacob when she poses as Rachel on their wedding day, leading to a hatred so deep that Jacob planned to divorce her.[57] God blesses her with pregnancy, preventing this eventuality. Nahmanides explains that God "saw" the hatred but knew that Leah's motivation was pure:

56. Sforno on Genesis 29:31.

57. Genesis Rabba 71:2.

to be married to this righteous man and become part of the creation of the Jewish people.[58]

An alternative reading is that Leah is "hated" by the larger community, seen as a laughingstock who could only get married by tricking someone. Her pregnancy is proof to the world, and to Jacob,[59] that she is worthy of becoming a mother of the nation.

Once Esau loses his claim to be one of the forefathers, based on the poor decisions he makes, the woman who was predestined to be his wife finds herself in a difficult predicament. When Jacob receives Esau's blessing through trickery, he receives Leah, Esau's predestined wife, by trickery as well. In the morning, when Jacob discovers the exchange, he says to Leah, "All night I was calling you Rachel and you answered. Why did you deceive me?" Leah replies, "Because when your father called you Esau, you also responded."[60] The pot cannot call the kettle black.

Leah is able to change her fate. Once she determines Esau's true character, she prays and cries, weakening her eyes,[61] asking God not to place her in the home of an evil man. Her desire to be part of the building of the nation of Israel is so strong that she allows herself to be part of an elaborate deception, resulting in Jacob's antagonism toward her.[62]

Leah bears children, and their names represent her desire to earn Jacob's love: Reuben ("God has seen my affliction. Now my husband will love me" – Gen. 29:32); Shimon ("God has heard that I am unloved, so He has given me this son also" – Gen. 29:33); and Levi ("Now that I have borne him three sons, my husband will walk with me" – Gen. 29:34). All of these names depict Leah's pain and suffering. Not only barren women suffer. Leah gives birth to a fourth son, Judah ("This time I will praise God" – Gen. 29:35). She understands that she has birthed more than her fair share of Jacob's sons.[63]

58. Nahmanides on Genesis 29:31.
59. Genesis Rabba 71:2.
60. Ibid. 70:19.
61. Ibid. 70:16.
62. Rabbi Joseph B. Soloveitchik, *Yemei Zikaron* [Hebrew] (Sifriat Elinar, 1986), 61–66.
63. Genesis Rabba 71:4

Leah realizes that she has stopped having children and follows her sister in giving her maidservant, Zilpah, to Jacob (Gen. 30:9). Zilpah gives birth to two sons, Gad and Asher, both names expressing luck (Gen. 30:11–13). The choice of names indicates to us that at this point, Leah is happy and almost secure in her position as mother of the majority of Jacob's children. This will give her an undeniable advantage and prestige in the home, where a wife's standing is based on her ability to bring healthy children into the world. This explains why she gives her maidservant to Jacob, even though she was certainly not barren. She understands that her position is directly connected to the continued delivery of Jacob's offspring. We see from Leah's response to Rachel during the incident with the mandrakes[64] that she views herself as Jacob's primary wife, exclaiming to her, "Is it not enough that you have taken my husband?" (Gen. 30:15). Leah and Rachel make a trade for the plants, and Leah bears two more sons to Jacob, Issachar and Zebulun (Gen. 30:17–20).[65]

Leah represents strength. She has a glimpse of her destiny, and with all her might, she fights it and takes back control. She knows what she wants and does what is necessary to achieve it.

RACHEL

Jacob meets Rachel, falls in love with her, and serves Laban for fourteen years in order to marry her.

Like Sarah and Rebecca, Rachel is clearly identified as a barren woman (Gen. 29:31). In a play on words, the Midrash states that although Rachel is barren, *akara*, she is the *ikar habayit*, the prominent personality in Jacob's household.[66] When the two sisters are mentioned in the

64. In Genesis 30:14–16, Reuben finds mandrakes in the field and brings them to his mother Leah. Rachel asks if she can have some of them, as they are believed to be a fertility aid. In the end, Rachel gives Leah her own night with Jacob in exchange for the mandrakes.
65. These brothers are successful in creating the partnership that Jacob and Esau did not build.
66. Genesis Rabba 71:2.

Book of Ruth, Rachel's name precedes that of her older sister Leah, even among Leah's descendants (Ruth 4:11).

The verse tells us that when Rachel realizes that she is barren, she becomes jealous of Leah, and tells Jacob that if he doesn't give her children, she will die (Gen. 30:1). This dramatic statement demonstrates the devastating pain of a barren woman who feels that there is no meaning in her life and has no will to continue.

How is it that Rachel, who was willing to do the impossible for her sister, is suddenly jealous of her? The Midrash explains that Rachel is jealous of Leah's virtuous actions, proof that Leah is more righteous and therefore deserving of pregnancy.[67] Meanwhile, Jacob's harsh response, "Am I in place of God?" surprises us. Where is his compassion for the woman he loves? The Midrash deduces that indeed, Jacob is later punished for this insensitivity.[68]

Like Sarah, Rachel gives her maid, Bilhah, to Jacob, hoping to "build a family through her" (Gen. 30:3). This may be an act of repentance for her jealousy; not only does Rachel overcome this negative trait, but she now allows and even encourages her husband to take another wife. Rachel's maid delivers two sons, their names also a window into Rachel's world: Dan ("God has vindicated me. He has listened to my voice and given me a son" – Gen. 30:6) and Naftali ("I have struggled hard with my sister and I have won" – Gen. 30:8). Rachel views these sons as her own and names them herself, revealing the desire, pain, and jealousy she experienced. The name Dan comes from judgment; Rachel accepts God's harsh judgment of barrenness. Through introspection, she realizes that it was not in Jacob's hands. It was purely from God. The name Naftali is not necessarily a negative reflection of Rachel's relationship with her sister, but rather denotes a new connection to other mothers, a bond that she could never have as a barren woman.

Reuben, Leah's first son, brings mandrakes from the field to his mother. Rachel asks Leah for some of the flowers, and eventually trades them for her evening with Jacob (Gen. 30:14–16). According to various commentators, these plants were viewed as medical aids for conception.

---

67. Ibid. 71:9.
68. Ibid. 71:7.

In desperation, Rachel trades physical intimacy with her husband, grasping at straws in order to conceive. The birth of the sons through her maidservant still doesn't fulfill her own desire to conceive, but she makes a poor choice in this event.[69] She gets the flowers, but Leah conceives Issachar and Zebulun.

Afterward, God remembers Rachel and He opens her womb (Gen. 30:22). Why now? At this point, ten of Jacob's twelve sons have been born and Leah turns to God and begs Him to give Rachel a child.[70] The circle is now complete: Rachel saved Leah from embarrassment, and now Leah saves Rachel from the same. Rashi suggests that Rachel was afraid that if she was barren, she would be sent from Jacob's home and end up with Esau, just as Leah had feared.[71] Rachel names her child Joseph, saying, "God has taken away my shame" (Gen. 30:23), in the hopes that she will have another son (Gen. 30:24).

While the family begins to return to the Land of Israel, Rachel goes into labor and dies in childbirth at the age of thirty-seven,[72] after discovering that she has birthed a boy whom she names Ben Oni (literally, "the son of my suffering"). Jacob renames him Benjamin (Gen. 35:16–20).

Rachel is buried on the road and her position there serves an important purpose. Years later, when the Jews are exiled, they are able to pass by her grave and pray. Rachel is heralded as one whose petitions before God are accepted. It is said that during the destruction of the Temple, the forefathers and foremothers tried to defend the Jewish people, but to no avail. Rachel then came before God and said, "You know how difficult it was for me when I thought I was to be married but instead Laban decided to put Leah in my place. Yet I, a human being, was not jealous and gave my sister the signs so she would not be humiliated." God answered, "Yes, Rachel, cease your crying. There is a reward for your actions. Your sons will return to their land."[73]

69. Genesis Rabba 72:3 states that Rachel is not buried with Jacob as a result of trading away her night with him.
70. *Tanḥuma, Vayetzeh* 8.
71. Rashi on Genesis 22:30.
72. *Seder Olam Rabba* 82.
73. *Pesikta Eikha Rabba* 24.

When Rachel gave Leah the signs to trick Jacob into thinking she was Rachel, she put herself in an impossible situation. It is against Torah law for a man to marry two sisters. The forefathers kept all of Torah before it was given,[74] but only in the Land of Israel.[75] This meant that when they entered the land, the sister who Jacob married second could not go with them.

Rachel's character trait is kindness, demonstrated by her willingness to give the signs to her sister. Jacob, once he received Esau's blessing, has two main character traits: strength and kindness, which together with love, beauty, and harmony fuse into *Tiferet*. *Tiferet*, the sixth of the ten kabbalistic *sefirot*, integrates kindness and strength to create a necessary balance between these two characteristics. Hence, Jacob needs both Rachel and Leah in order to reach perfection.[76]

74. Mishna Kiddushin 4:14.
75. Nahmanides on Genesis 26:5.
76. Rabbi Joseph B. Soloveitchik, *Yemei Zikaron* [Hebrew] (Sifriat Elinar, 1986), 61–66.

Leah's Story: Trial by Water

By Leah V. Herzog

At the beginning of my marriage, going to the *mikve* felt like a privilege and a gift. I embraced the experience for all its spirituality. This was a woman's mitzva, and I felt so proud to be able to do it. The water represented so many things to me: the primordial waters of *Bereshit,* Miriam's well, rebirth, joy, life itself. As I went into the *mikve,* I sometimes felt tears of joy and awe well up in my eyes. I said each word of the *berakha* with my eyes closed, understanding the full meaning, and then immersed with open hands and a brimming heart. I felt myself preparing my *neshama* and my body for the new life that would grow. I said *tefillot* and *tehillim* and offered my own pleas to the Creator. I thought that if I did this mitzva right, if I had the purest and most proper *kavana,* then we would be blessed with a child.

Each month that I didn't get pregnant was a blow. The physical pain was a shadow of the psychological and spiritual pain. And each month, as I prepared for the *mikve,* I fought with myself. I grappled with doubt and anger. If I was following the rules, if I was doing what Hashem commanded me to do, why wasn't I having children? My next thoughts often went like this: *This is my* yetzer hara *and I can't listen to it! Hashem only sends us* nisyonot *that we can handle.* That was followed by: *Hashem wants your* tefillot, *just like He wanted those of the* Imahot. But that midrash either rang hollow and cruel in my ears, or it shot arrows of guilt through me. *Who do you think you are, comparing yourself to the* Imahot?

I saw the *Avot* and *Imahot* as role models. My Hebrew name is Leah, and when I was eighteen, I was diagnosed with an incurable eye disease. Somewhere in the back of my mind, as I grappled with coming to terms with a lifelong degenerative vision impairment, I had the following thought: *Well, if I am like Leah in having weak eyes, at least I will also be like Leah in having a lot of children.*

I had always wanted to be a mother. I imagined having children before I thought about being married. I don't really know where that deep maternal instinct and yearning came from. Perhaps it was because I was lonely. I was an awkward kid, I didn't have many friends, and my three half-siblings were ten, twelve, and fourteen years older than I (and they didn't marry until much later). Perhaps it was because I was a child of survivors, and I was trained from a young age to take care of my mother. Perhaps it was because I was born in Tammuz – the astrological sign of the crab is associated with nurturing. When I was little, my dolls and stuffed animals were my babies. By the time I was twelve, I was babysitting. I was the girl who was always holding someone's kid, the girl who wanted to be a kindergarten teacher when she grew up.

I loved being Jewish and when I was a teenager, I became observant. Orthodox Judaism provided – and continues to provide – three vital things for me: a set of rules connected to a higher purpose, a sense of community, and a source of meaning and spirituality. I'm a *Yekke* by birth, upbringing, and temperament, so rules are important to me. On the other hand, I am a Hasid in my *neshama*, and I very much wanted to belong to something. The concepts of *hashgaḥa pratit*, *sekhar ve'onesh*, and fidelity to Hashem, Torah, and mitzvot resonated deeply, and I firmly believed that if I did what was right and true, my dream of becoming a wife and mother would be fulfilled.

I am deeply cognizant of the *ḥesed* that Hashem did for me in sending me the man who became my husband, who was completely undeterred by my diagnosis, and whose desires to have a large family matched my own. We talked happily about having six, seven, even ten kids. We were young when we married – twenty-one and twenty-four – and we were blissfully naive.

Before my wedding, a woman whom I had been close to since I was a teenager called me up and told me some of her own story. "Do you remember the big thermometer you once saw in my bathroom?" she asked me. "I needed to take my temperature every day because we were trying to have children. I'm telling you this because one in six couples has infertility issues. I just want you to know. I hope you don't ever need this information, but I wanted to make sure that someone told you."

This knowledge was another *ḥesed*. Our infertility journey was long and painful. It took us nine years to have our son; we started treatments after fourteen months of marriage.

As time wore on, and we were immersed in infertility treatments that were exhausting, wreaked havoc with my hormones, emptied our bank account, and exhausted our souls, I wondered whether Hashem was even listening or caring. Besides, I already had one *nisayon* – my deteriorating vision. Wasn't that enough?

After almost four years, I became pregnant for the first time. Fear lurked under the joy, and indeed, the pregnancy ended with a traumatic stillbirth at thirty-two weeks. I closed myself off from Hashem. It wasn't that I lost my *emuna*; rather, I had no interest in having a conversation with the *Boreh Olam*. I was a Torah teacher, we lived an observant life, I went to *shul*. At home, in *shul*, and in the *mikve*, along with my *tefillot* for children, I now also davened to find my way back to Hashem. I delved into the lives of the women in Tanakh, so many of whom struggled with infertility, and I tried to emulate them. They were not saints. Each one displayed anger and despair in her own way. Their humanity was what inspired me and gave me hope. I never stopped fighting with myself not to become bitter, to keep trying, to find joy, to be involved with other people and their families. I spent time in nature and reveled at the almost indescribable beauty of Hashem's universe. I wrote, I played instruments, I learned Torah and worked on my doctorate.

I very consciously chose life. Gradually, the door that I had closed but never locked began to open again.

Our son was born after almost nine years. I named him after my father. Like the biblical Leah, my firstborn's name is Reuven. Like Leah, I felt that Hashem had seen my suffering and given us a son. The alternate way to read the name Reuven also rang true for us: *Re'u! Ben!* – Look! A son!

There was another disastrous pregnancy, which ended with miscarrying twins. This time, I found my way back through Malbim's introduction to the book of Job. According to one opinion, Job was written by Moses, as he too grappled with the unknowable. As I stared into the waters of the *mikve,* which still reminded me of the original waters and of life itself, I thought of what Hashem finally said to Job: "Were you there when I created the universe?" I realized that I needed to learn to live with *emuna* alone. There would never be any answers.

A little over a year after the miscarriage, almost four years after our son was born and twelve and a half years after we married, Hashem answered us and we had our daughter, Eliana.

We have two children, not ten or even six. We have a boy and a girl. They are healthy, bright, wonderful human beings who bring us great joy. And while I realize that Hashem's rules are as unfathomable as the deepest waters, I also know that like the *Imahot* before me, I have *emuna.*

Leah V. Herzog, M.Ed., spent thirty years teaching high school students and adults in the US and now lives in Israel, where she is a senior educator at The Lookstein Center at Bar-Ilan University. Leah is also a writer, a tour guide for the Bible Lands Museum Jerusalem, and a mentor for people dealing with vision impairment and reproductive challenges.

Chapter 2

Hazlelponi

The Day of Tidings

For a long while the dreadful enemy
brought Samaria to siege;
four lepers to her brought tidings.
To her brought the tidings of freedom.

A Samaria under siege – the entire land,
the famine is too hard to bear.
But I will not want news of freedom,
if it comes from the mouth of a leper.

The pure will bring news and the pure will redeem,
and if his hand won't be there to redeem –
then I will choose to die from the suffering of the siege
on the eve of the great day of tidings.

Rachel Bluwstein, 1927

In this poem based on II Kings 7, the poet Rachel Bluwstein mocks those who refuse to accept redemption when it is not brought about in the way they envisioned. The poet utilizes this biblical story to draw a parallel to those who did not approve of the early Zionists due to their lack of religious practices. The clear implication is that God has many messengers, and though they may not look like we imagined, and they may even be "impure as lepers," our challenge is to recognize God's emissaries and accept their missive. God sends the call through the messengers who are most appropriate for that generation.

The Cycle of the Judges

In the book of Judges, we see a repetitive cycle throughout the stories. There is a sin, usually idol worship. Then God sends an enemy to subjugate and punish the people. The nation turns to God with supplication and prayer, leading to salvation.[1] Chapter 13 begins with a description of continued sin by the Jewish people and their subsequent subjugation to the new enemy, the Philistines, for forty years, a period of time that indicates two generations. The people have been living in this reality for as long as they remember. Surprisingly, the next verse begins to describe the birth of Samson, who will save the people. But the supplication is missing. This is a clear exception to the general pattern of the book.

Why does God decide to send redemption without the people repenting? Suffering usually induces the people to "return," to repent, but if after so many years the people have not been moved, the plan is not working. God decides to try something else. God is going to save the people, but not by the usual means. Samson is a problematic leader who uses questionable methods to achieve success.

Manoah and His Wife

We are introduced to Manoah from the tribe of Dan, who lives in Tzora[2] with his barren, anonymous wife. An angel appears to the woman informing her that she will give birth to a son who will save the people. Unlike many of the infertile couples who prayed or took second wives in an effort to change their lot, this couple remains passive. Just as the

1. See Menachem Leibtag, Shiurim on Chumash and Navi, available at: https://tanach.org/navi/SHOF3.TXT.
2. Near present-day Beit Shemesh.

nation does not turn to God to save them, this childless couple does not beseech God for a child. The barren couple represents the dry, empty nation. God sends a son and a savior without supplication.

Following this introduction, we might expect Manoah to be the main character. But as his name insinuates (it is rooted in the Hebrew verb "to rest"), he is secondary to his more dominant and righteous wife. Although in rabbinic literature, Manoah is grouped together with notable men such as Elkanah, Jesse, and Boaz, the angel does not appear to him, only to his wife, and not once but twice.[3] Manoah is considered a simpleton in the Gemara (Arakhin 18b) since he "follows after his wife" (Judges 13:11).

Biblical society was patriarchal; a woman's identity was tied to a male: her father, husband, or brother. Most biblical women are unnamed. The Bible names 1,426 men and only 177 women, so that women constitute just 12.4 percent of the names that appear in the Bible.[4] Although Manoah's wife is clearly the superior personality in the story (hence the angel appears to her), she remains unnamed. Using the law of conservation of biblical personalities,[5] the Sages identify her as Hazlelponi (Bava Batra 91a). In II Chronicles 4:3 we meet a woman from Tzora who is named, but no other information is given about her. Since it is unusual for a woman in the Bible to be mentioned by name at all, we can assume that she has some significance. The Sages take the anonymous woman from our episode in the book of Judges and associate her with the named but unidentified woman in II Chronicles. Her name comes from the root Z-L-L, a possible reference to angels, "shadows of God"[6] whom she met twice.

The Midrash on the book of Proverbs associates each sentence of the *Eshet Ḥayil* (Woman of Valor) song with a different biblical female

3. Numbers Rabba 10:5.
4. Prof. Uriel Simon, "*Vayelekh Manoaḥ Aḥarei Ishto*," available at: https://daat.ac.il/daat/tanach/tora/simon1-1.htm.
5. According to the law of conservation of biblical personalities, different characters in Tanakh may be linked with each other. In some cases, an unnamed character is said to be a certain well-known character. In other cases, two well-known characters are said to be the same person.
6. Numbers Rabba 10:5.

character, so that the song is a reference to twenty different women instead of a single woman. The verse "She makes bedcoverings for herself; linen and purple is her garment" (Prov. 31:22) is said to reference Hazlelponi,[7] who weaves, then sells her product, raises her child, and teaches Torah in the market in a very clear manner.[8] This approach provides her with a number of talents unmentioned in the text: business acumen and education, both within her family and beyond. It seems the Midrash wants to characterize Samson's mother as a distinguished woman.

The Angel's First Appearance

The angel, on his first appearance to Hazlelponi, delivers some important information. He begins by telling her that she is barren (Judges 13:3) but will give birth to a son. Therefore, she needs to be careful not to drink wine or eat anything unclean,[9] as the child will be a nazirite who will save the Israelites from their enemies (Judges 13:4–5). Like a number of other biblical barren women, she receives the news of the miraculous birth of the future redeemer along with some restrictions. The biblical nazirite is not allowed to have contact with any substance derived from grapes, cut his hair, or come in contact with dead bodies. This third limitation was not applicable to Samson in his role as military rescuer.[10] God's commandment that Samson would have the status of a nazirite from birth was a way of trying to rein in Samson and control his power.

---

7. *Midrash Eshet Ḥayil*, vol. 2, 149.
8. This last explanation comes from the fact that the Hebrew root Z-L-L, "clear," is found in the name Hazlelponi.
9. It is unclear why the angel emphasizes that she must not eat anything unclean. Isn't this the law regardless? One explanation is that many people at that time were not careful regarding these laws, so the special mention was necessary. A second explanation is that this was included among the other restrictions that apply to a nazirite.
10. Maimonides, *Sefer Hafla'a, Hilkhot Nezirut* 3:13.

The woman does not react to the angel – she does not question or laugh. She simply runs to tell her husband.

Informing Manoah

The reader does not know how many years the couple has been barren. When the woman goes to share the news with Manoah, she describes the messenger as an awe-inspiring man of God, like a divine angel, of whom she asked no questions. She does not deliver the information the same way she received it, perhaps thinking that her husband might not believe her, or in order to explain why she was the one to receive the message. First, she leaves out the fact that she is the reason that they have not had children.[11] Perhaps this was a sensitive point in their relationship, and in ancient times there was no way to know which spouse was barren, unless the husband had children with a second wife. She leaves out the details of what it means to be a nazirite, such as the restriction on cutting hair, since this was known, and she omits the fact that their son will be the savior of the Israelites. Maybe she leaves it out in order to protect Samson. Once two people know a fact it's no longer a secret, and it could be dangerous for the child. Or perhaps she does not want to influence the way he will be educated and raised. She may even have thought it was obvious, given the divine tidings of his birth. She may also have thought that she received the visit from the angel because the particulars of what she could eat were relevant only to her, not Manoah.

Her description of the messenger and the fact that she didn't question him make the information more believable, and it preempts her husband's questioning nature. It seems that the angel appeared to her because she was more accepting and would be open to receiving the news.[12]

Manoah has a choice regarding whether to believe the message his wife brings. He wishes the angel had appeared to him,[13] so he prays to God that the "man" should reappear to explain what will be with the

11. Numbers Rabba 10.
12. Abrabanel on Judges 13.
13. Josephus, *Antiquities of the Jews* 2:44.

child (Judges 13:8). Manoah is asking to be involved as well. He didn't pray for his wife to bear a child, but now he prays?

The Angel's Second Appearance

God listens to Manoah but sends the angel back to the woman a second time (Judges 13:9). She hurries to her husband to inform him of the man's reappearance. While she rushes, indicating her desire to maintain her husband's dignity, Manoah himself does not rush (Judges 13:10). Is he disappointed that the messenger did not appear to him? Now that the angel has returned, but not in the way Manoah desired, his lack of enthusiasm is apparent.

Manoah, after checking that the "man" is indeed the messenger, asks for clarity about the child. His questions are legitimate, focusing on why this child needs to be announced, and why he needs to be a nazirite from birth. The angel could have repeated his original message to Manoah's wife, but instead he includes her adaptations, leaving out the details of her barrenness, the restriction on cutting the child's hair, and the fact that the child will be the people's savior. The angel does not add any new information, and therefore does not actually answer Manoah's questions.

Manoah Makes an Offering

In Genesis, Abraham offers food to his angel guests before they deliver their message. Now Manoah seeks to pay respects to his visitor in the form of a meal. While his wife does not volunteer anything, it seems that Manoah is trying to make himself important. The angel says that he cannot eat their food, but suggests an offering instead. Since the couple has just received wonderful news, the offering is appropriate as a form of thanksgiving,[14] but it could also be Manoah's way of trying to determine who is standing in front of him. Manoah asks for the visitor's name (Judges 13:17), claiming that he needs to know it in order to pay him the proper respect. In contrast to Hazlelponi, who is accepting of

14. Numbers Rabba 10.

and open to God's message, Manoah remains skeptical and needs reassurance that this is indeed a message from God. The angel answers that his name is Peli, which is either connected to the future child's nazirite status or means that the name is hidden or too wondrous to tell.[15]

Two of our three main characters are nameless. Both the woman and the angel are not identified, putting them together on a different level than Manoah.

Going Up in Smoke

Manoah begins to offer the sacrifice, and as the flames rise, the messenger disappears in the flames. Manoah understands that the messenger was a divine angel, and he and his wife fall to the floor, humbling themselves and showing respect. Manoah fears that they will die as a result of seeing an angel from God. Hazlelponi points out that if God was going to take their lives, He would not have sent them a message about the birth of a child.

We see completely different reactions: from the outset, the woman's reaction is one of belief and acceptance, while the man is cynical and filled with doubt. It is only once the miracle is over and the angel has disappeared that Manoah understands the magnitude of what he has just experienced, but by then it is too late. The event has finished and the angel will not return.[16] Manoah misses the opportunity to recognize God's messenger.

The Birth of Samson

The child is born and his mother names him Samson. His name reflects the protection that he gives his generation, much like the sun that sustains all living things (Sota 10a).

---

15. Ibid. 10:15
16. Dr. Nili Samet, "The Secret of Manoah's Wife: On the Biblical Characterization of an Outstanding Personality," available at: https://www.yutorah.org/sidebar/lecture.cfm/746095/dr-nili-samet/the-secret-of-manoah-s-wife-on-the-biblical-characterization-of-an-outstanding-personality/.

Aside from telling the story of a miraculous birth, this chapter teaches the importance of being open to the messages of God whenever they come, regardless of the messenger. Redemption will always occur, though not necessarily in the way we have hoped.

Chapter 3

Hannah

The Charge to Create

The familiar *Anim Zemirot* poem sung at the end of Shabbat morning prayers proclaims that "God showed Moses the knot of His tefillin." Rabbi Aryeh Kaplan explains that when a Jewish man dons tefillin, he is striving to imitate God. He suggests that women do not need external props such as tefillin to imitate God, as they have an inherent godliness, which is manifested in their ability to procreate. Women possess certain heavenly attributes that men, and even angels, do not.

On the simplest level, mitzvot establish a link with God. The most profound way to connect with God is by emulating Him. Women resemble God in a way that no man could ever hope to do – only a woman can create within her body; only a woman can bear a child. In this sense, a woman may embody some of God's attributes more intimately than any man. The kabbalists teach us that the hand-tefillin represent this feminine element. The hollow center of the tefillin box represents the womb, and the coils wrapped around the arm represent the umbilical cord. What a man signifies with an object, a woman achieves with her very body. The box portion of the tefillin is called a *bayit*, literally, a house. A woman has her own *bayit*: the home in which she raises her family. One could say that a woman's home is her tefillin.[1]

1. Aryeh Kaplan, "Tefillin," in *The Aryeh Kaplan Anthology* 2 (Mesorah Publications), 273.

Rabbi Kaplan's poignant, thought-provoking idea challenges both men and women to imitate and emulate our Creator.

Imitatio Dei

Man was created in God's image (Gen. 1:21). This simple declaration has mystified generations of commentators. How can mortal man ever hope to be like an infinite God? How can corporeal humans approach God, who has no physical properties? Further, why is it important to be like God? What can be achieved by being like God?

Man's ability to emulate God fosters his connection to God. What makes this even a possibility is that God created man in His image. This idea is instructive as well as beneficial. As it says in *Ethics of the Fathers*:

> He used to say: Beloved is man, for he was created in the image of God; it is by special divine love that he is informed that he was created in the image of God. As it is stated: "For God made man in His own image."[2]

Rashi contends that through man's cognitive faculties, we are able to imitate God.[3] Maimonides clarifies that it is this quality that distinguishes humans from the rest of God's creations.[4] Alternatively, the *Meshekh Ḥokhma* suggests that it is our free will that mirrors God; just as God can choose to do anything, so too man is given the opportunity to select any path he wishes to pursue.[5] Rabbi Eliyahu Dessler offers another opinion, interpreting "the image of God" as the innate morality common to all mankind.[6]

---

2. Mishna Avot 3:14.
3. Rashi on Genesis 1:21.
4. Introduction, *Commentary on the Mishna* 17:20.
5. *Meshekh Ḥokhma* on Genesis 1:21.
6. *Mikhtav MeEliyahu* 1:32.

God's Attributes

God sets forth His qualities in the Torah (Ex. 34). These verses serve as the source and blueprint for how man should mirror God, including attributes such as compassion and graciousness. The Talmud addresses this point and declares: "God is merciful, dresses the naked, visits the sick, comforts mourners.... Man's life goal should be to make every effort to emulate his Creator" (Sota 14a).

Man's limitations preclude him from performing positive acts on the scale and scope of a deity. Nonetheless, man is obliged to emulate God's attributes in his interactions with his fellow man. When man adopts these characteristics, he may credibly petition God to act reciprocally toward him (Shabbat 127b). Maimonides argues that refining one's personality with the godly traits of compassion, graciousness, and righteousness defines our obligation to be like God.[7]

Creator

Thus far we have presented the well-known interpretation that man can fulfill the seemingly difficult commandment to "be like God" by emulating God's attributes. Rabbi Joseph B. Soloveitchik offers a fresh perspective. In his view, it is man's creative abilities that enable him to be like God.[8] There is no doubt that the term "image of God" in the first account of Creation (Gen. 1) refers to man's inner force as a creative being. Man's likeness to God expresses itself in his determination and ability to create. Adam, the first man fashioned in the image of God, was blessed with great drive for creative activity and immeasurable resources for the realization of this goal.

Rabbi Soloveitchik argues that creativity is manifest in the form of physical inventions such as bridges, railroads, and starts-ups, and in the spiritual realm with innovations in Torah, philosophy, and morality. These original ideas contain an element of creation *ex nihilo,* something from nothing, corresponding with God's creation of the world. It is said

7. *Sefer HaMitzvot,* Positive Commandment 8.
8. Rabbi Joseph B. Soloveitchik, "The Lonely Man of Faith," *Tradition* (Summer 1965): 9.

that God did not completely finish the world; rather, He left it unfinished so that mankind could partner with Him in its creation.

Hannah and Rosh HaShana

In the Rosh HaShana service, God is referred to as the Creator. Rosh HaShana is the day that God created the world and annually judges all of His creations.[9] If man's ultimate goal is to emulate God, then it follows that on this day he should strive to be creative. Rabbi Soloveitchik expands on this idea:

> The Torah describes Creation at length in order to teach us a very important lesson – "to walk in all His ways" – and to instruct man to imitate his Creator and to himself become a creator. A person should not shake his head, saying that this demand of man is impossible. After all, he cannot imitate his Creator in creativity. At most, he can adopt some element of His other traits – loving-kindness, mercy, and the like. Nevertheless, the Torah demands of man and commands him to tirelessly exert himself to cling to the traits of the Holy One, blessed be He, and to be a creator like Him.[10]

On Rosh HaShana, we read the first chapter of the book of Samuel (Megilla 31a). The Gemara explains that this is because Hannah was "remembered" on this day as God accepted her prayers and granted her wish to conceive (Rosh HaShana 11a).

The Narrative

The reader is introduced to Elkanah, who has two wives: Peninnah, who has children, and Hannah, who is barren. Every year, Elkanah and his family travel to the *Mishkan* in Shiloh to offer sacrifices. He distributes portions of the sacrifice to Peninnah and their children, and as an expression of his love, he gives a special, larger portion to Hannah. Every year,

9. See the prayer *HaYom Harat Olam* in the Rosh HaShana service.
10. Rabbi Joseph B. Soloveitchik, *Yemei Zikaron* [Hebrew] (Sifriat Elinar, 1986), 86.

Peninnah taunts Hannah, leading to an anguished Hannah tearfully refusing to eat. Hannah does not respond to the provocations directed at her, as she tacitly accepts that her barrenness is ordained from Heaven.

On one occasion, Elkanah expresses concern over Hannah's heartache, claiming that his love for her exceeds that of even ten sons. Elkanah's declaration motivates Hannah to eat and drink. She then proceeds to the *Mishkan* and pours out her heart to God in prayer. According to Malbim, until Elkanah downplayed her misery, she presumed that he was praying for her.[11] Now that she understands that she is on her own and that her pain is not his, she throws herself into her prayers.

The Pivot

Elkanah's remark, although most likely unintentional, jars Hannah like a clap of thunder as she suddenly understands that she is alone in her heartbreaking plight. No one else can alleviate her torment. Like an abandoned soldier behind enemy lines, the only place she can find resolution is within. Hannah searches the innermost recesses of her essence in order to extricate herself from her untenable, hopeless position and move forward. Typically, and crucially, the hero's response to the difficult predicament needs to be correct and on point. A misstep at the critical instant can lead to the soldier's capture, the refugee's failure, or the patient's demise. No one would have faulted Hannah if she had simply thrown up her hands in frustration and grudgingly accepted her sad fate. Her realization that "it depends on me alone" propels her to reassess her situation and place her unique, original stamp on history. She finds God's image within, and takes the immediate and appropriate response, directly and sincerely appealing to God in the *Mishkan*, the holiest of places, in her unique and singular way.

Hannah as Originator

The novelty of Hannah's supplication provides the key to understanding her character, and explains God's positive response to her desperate

11. Malbim on I Samuel 1:9.

plea. Hannah successfully uses her innate divine image (*tzelem Elokim*) to emulate God by being spiritually creative. She is then able to be physically creative – in the most literal sense – by bearing a child. Hannah's originality and creativity manifest in several ways:

Prayer

Hannah's seminal prayer service is so groundbreaking that generations of Jewish legislators, commentators, and philosophers have dissected its style and substance, drawing numerous lessons about one of the most central elements of the religious experience. It is from this episode that the Gemara derives the essential laws of prayer (Berakhot 31), and indeed, every formal Jewish prayer to this day is patterned after Hannah's fateful burst of inspiration at Shiloh.

Hannah was the creator of the silent prayer, characterized by moving lips and no sound. The content of the silent *Amida* also correlates with Hannah's prayer, as all the blessings inserted in this official, standardized prayer centuries later by the Men of the Great Assembly appear in her heartfelt prayer.[12] Further paralleling Hannah's prayer, the Men of the Great Assembly instituted nine blessings in the Rosh HaShana Musaf prayer. The Midrash asserts that women, who are normally exempt from positive, time-bound commandments such as prayer (Berakhot 20b), are nonetheless obligated to recite the *Amida* because of the gender connection to Hannah. It is clear that Hannah is the innovator, creator – one could even say mother – of the doctrine of Jewish prayer.

Conceptually, Hannah teaches the appropriate frame of mind for prayer. Eli, the high priest, perceives her silent mutterings as alcohol induced. In a sense, she *is* drunk – from her spiritual experience. Hannah creates the idea that one can allow prayer to completely overwhelm one's consciousness.

Every prayer has its own unique quality. The Midrash assigns each verse in Proverbs to a different biblical female character, and it associates the verse "When she discerns that her wares are good, her lamp is not extinguished by night" (Prov. 31:18) with Hannah.[13] The Hebrew

12. *Yalkut Shimoni* on I Samuel, *remez* 80.
13. *Midrash Mishlei* 31.

word used here for "advises" is *taama*, meaning "she tastes/discerns." The association with Hannah alludes to her tasting the flavor of prayer. Similarly, the *Nefesh HaḤayim* comments:

> And when a person sends out vaporous breaths and words during his prayer, a number of winged creatures spread their wings and mouths to receive them; this is what is written: "For a bird of the heavens will carry the sound and one who has wings..." (Eccl. 10:20). And the Holy One, blessed be He, accepts those words, and with them builds worlds, as is written in relation to them (Is. 66:22): "For just as the new heavens and the new earth..." and [in relation to] the secret of the word: "and I have placed My words in your mouth...to plant the heavens...'" (Is. 51:16). [And regarding the verse] "And to say to Zion, 'You are My people,'" don't read it as *ami*, "My people," but rather as *imi*, "with Me," My partner.[14]

Hannah's form of prayer is so original and unrecognizable that Eli accuses her of being drunk. What he fails to realize is that she is imbibed with passion for God, not alcohol. Does he not recognize her from previous visits? Doesn't he appreciate her deep anguish? Hannah answers him respectfully even though he coldly mocks her.

Promise

Many biblical personalities interact with God through prayer,[15] while others take personal oaths.[16] There is a problematic element of hubris in an oath, as it is presumptuous for a human to "cut a deal" with God. Hannah's oath, however, has a significant distinction in that she promises to dedicate the very object of her prayers to God. In addition, by coupling the two elements of prayer and oath, Hannah effectively

14. *Nefesh HaḤayim* 2:10.
15. See Genesis 18:23 (Abraham), Genesis 25:21 (Isaac), and Exodus 32:31 and Deuteronomy 3:23 (Moses).
16. See Genesis 28:20 (Jacob), Numbers 21:2 (Israelite nation), and Judges 11:29 (Jephthah).

removes any tinge of pretentiousness. She modestly refers to herself as "Your maidservant" three times. The Gemara suggests that in doing so, she is referring to the three mitzvot given to women: lighting Shabbat candles, tithing *ḥalla*, and observing the laws of family purity (Berakhot 31a). The insinuation is that if women do not observe these laws, they will be punished, and Hannah alludes to these mitzvot in order to affirm that she has scrupulously adhered to all of them and therefore does not deserve to be immured in the prison of infertility and sadness. Indeed, Hannah's name is an acronym for these laws: *ḥet – ḥalla, nun – nidda* (laws of family purity), *heh – hadlakat nerot* (lighting Shabbat candles).

Hannah creates a new type of devotional service which blends prayer and oath in a single formulation. There are numerous examples throughout Tanakh of prayer, and there are numerous examples of oaths, but Hannah is the first to combine them.

Hannah learns from her ancestor, Jacob, how to make a vow. On his way to Laban, Jacob promises God that if he returns home safely, he will build God a temple (Gen. 28:20). Hannah proposes a similar idea, dedicating her future child to the service of God (I Sam. 1:11). In doing so, Hannah creates the amalgamation of prayer and promise.

Naziritism

A further expression of Hannah's creativity is her commitment to offer her future child as a nazirite.[17] While Hannah's declaration may be well intentioned, Radak questions the vow's validity,[18] as the object of her oath is not extant, and it also runs counter to the Mishna's ruling that a woman cannot sanctify her child as a nazirite (Nazir 28b).

The Sages become absorbed with the legalities of Hannah's vow, giving little attention to several key issues: What happens if the child refuses or is not fit to serve? Can children be browbeaten into follow-

17. The only other person in Tanakh to be declared a nazirite before birth is Samson; that status is initiated by God. (The Gemara offers two opinions in Nazir 66a: R. Naharia uses a certain verse as proof that Samson and Samuel were both nazirites, while R. Yosei says that verse simply means that people would be afraid of Samuel.)
18. Radak on I Samuel 1:11.

ing a course if they have no interest in doing so? Can a parent compel their child to accept the parent's choices?

Rashi avoids the difficulties by claiming that Hannah's vow is essentially a prayer, as if to say, "I sincerely hope that my child will be an individual who is worthy of devoting his life to the service of God." This is a prayer rather than a vow, and when she returns years later to Shiloh with her son Samuel, she fulfills the prayer by famously declaring: "This is the boy I prayed for."[19] She also makes a personal commitment to encourage him to accept this goal by raising him in the right environment and surrounding him with these ideals. This is a pledge that she personally undertakes, not one that she takes on her son's behalf. Samuel must commit to the promise independently when he comes of age.[20]

Hannah is the first to consecrate her son as a potential nazirite. It also seems that Samuel's naziritism is unique: not only is it initiated by his mother; it is also only a partial naziritism that is limited to the prohibition of cutting hair but excludes the restrictions on drinking wine and coming into contact with the deceased. Eventually, Samuel does come in direct contact with a corpse, as he personally slays Agag in Gilgal (I Sam. 15:33). Naziritism is a complex issue that the Torah does not necessarily view in an entirely positive light (Num. 6:11). In her distinctive, innovative fashion, perhaps Hannah tries to create an original form of naziritism.

Name of God

In her prayer, Hannah addresses God as "Lord of Hosts." She is the creator of this appellation (Berakhot 31b). What is Hannah's intention in using this name? What is she referring to?

In ascribing to God this title, she alludes to His endless number of creations, suggesting that blessing her with one child would be a trivial task for Him. Alternatively, *Yalkut Shimoni* proposes that she is alluding to some of the fundamental differences between heavenly beings and

---

19. I Sam. 1:27.
20. And what did Elkanah think of all this? "Her husband Elkanah said to her, 'Do what seems best to you'" (I Sam. 1:23).

humans.[21] Celestial hosts, in contradistinction to their human counterparts, do not procreate or die. Hannah's plea emphasizes that she is mortal and is deserving of both the curse of death and the blessing of procreation, as if to say: "God, since I am a human who will eventually face the inevitable, unfortunate prospect of death, should You not also grant me the blessing of motherhood?" These explanations suggest that Hannah challenges God to bless her with a son either because it is a negligible task for God or because it is a basic feature of all humans.

According to Maimonides, there are seven names of God that demand respect, with Hannah's creation, "Lord of Hosts," being the seventh.[22] Each name represents a different attribute of God. The fact that Hannah successfully develops a lasting, descriptive title for God indicates her deep connection with Him and cements her as one of the most significant religious figures in Jewish history.

Hannah's request for a son is not for selfish reasons but for the glory of God. She pleads for a son who will have the potential to blossom into a leader and a messenger for God's sake. She has every intention of dedicating this child to God for his entire life. The idea of surrendering him to God does not indicate passivity; rather, it is creative, a demonstration of Hannah taking initiative.

After nearly twenty years of futility,[23] Hannah conceives and willingly presents her firstborn child to God.

In *Mesillat Yesharim,* the definition of a Hasid is twofold: it refers to someone whose every action is totally dedicated to the magnification of God's name, and to someone whose conduct is motivated by concern for the benefit and success of his entire generation.[24] Rabbi Shlomo Aviner contends that this was sorely lacking in Hannah and Elkanah's time, as God's presence was partially muted since there was no kingship proclaiming God's dominion in a forthright, public way.[25] The resultant desecration of God's name was deeply painful to Han-

21. *Yalkut Shimoni* on Samuel 1:1, s.v. *Amar.*
22. *Sefer HaMadda, Hilkhot Yesodei HaTorah* 6:1–2.
23. *Pesikta Rabbati* 43.
24. See chapter 19.
25. *Midrash Eshet Ḥayil,* 183.

nah. Her prayer demonstrates that her interest lies in having children who can help dispel this desecration of God's name by amplifying the knowledge of His presence in the world. Universal knowledge of God will be manifest once the Messianic Era is inaugurated by a descendant of King David, the sovereign crowned by Hannah's son Samuel.

This story vividly illustrates the crucial role that a preeminent person's background and surroundings play in his success. A parent's aspirations can have a profound impact on even the smallest of children (Samuel was only three years old when he began to serve in the *Mishkan*),[26] provided that these aspirations are accepted by the child and are not the result of selfish parental pressure that ignores the child's own wishes and needs. Despite the fact that the text omits the details of Samuel's upbringing, it is clear that Hannah was a master educator who was able to impart lofty Jewish ideals to her son. With his mother's instruction firmly penetrating his consciousness, Samuel fully accepts his mother's teachings and goals and devotes himself to serving God and the Jewish people. Subsequently, he becomes one of the greatest prophets in Jewish history, on par with Moses and Aaron (Berakhot 31b).

Monarchy

Samuel himself is an innovator who introduces Israel to the unprecedented concept of Jewish monarchy. Israel's first two kings, Saul and David, are both anointed by Samuel, and they both have a strong relationship with the prophet. The life of Samuel is recorded in a new book with new concepts and ideas, promoting new goals for the Israelite nation. Samuel plays an integral role in appointing a king and destroying Amalek, ultimately leading to the construction of the Temple.

26. See Rashi on 1 Samuel 1:22. Others believe he was probably older and explain that he was not weaned from nursing at this time, but weaned from needing a nanny.

Comparison to Rachel

Hannah and Rachel, both barren,[27] are married to men who have children from other women, yet they are the beloved wives.[28] Both feel threatened by the other woman,[29] but their husbands do not understand their distress.[30] God ultimately "remembers them"[31] and they bear offspring. They both name their sons in a way that reflects that the child is a gift from God.[32]

The reactions of these two childless women reflect their contrasting personalities. Rachel lashes out: She is jealous of her sister, angry at her husband, and does not turn to God. Rather, she gives her maidservants to her husband and then trades away a night with her husband in exchange for some flowers. Hannah, on the other hand, turns inward, becomes the originator of the prayer/oath model, creates a new name for God, and is blessed with a child which she promptly returns to God.

Hannah's second prayer is filled with gratitude, describing God's involvement in every part of life. Even though man partners with God and is gifted with the ability to create, Hannah reminds us that ultimately, everything is subject to God's will.

---

27. I Samuel 1:2; Genesis 29:31.
28. I Samuel 1:5; Genesis 29:30.
29. I Samuel 1:6; Genesis 30:8.
30. I Samuel 1:8; Genesis 30:2.
31. I Samuel 1:19; Genesis 30:22.
32. I Samuel 1:20; Genesis 30:23–24.

Chapter 4

The Shunamite Woman

The Last Dead of the Desert

Arise, desert wanderers, and leave the wilderness,
the road is long, the battles are many.

Cease your rootless drifting in the wasteland,
before you lies the great, open road.

Forty years we have wandered between the mountains –
six hundred thousand corpses we have buried in the sand.

Let not the corpses of the falterers delay us,
they died in slavery, let us pass over them!

They shall rot in their shame, sprawled over their parcels
carried on their shoulders from Egypt.

Let them dream pleasantly of onions, garlic,
huge tureens of meat.

Today or tomorrow the wind shall share
with the vulture the corpse of the last of the slaves.

Arise, therefore, wanderers! Leave the wilderness!

Haim Bialik, 1902

With these words, Haim Bialik calls upon even those who are dead, with no evident chance of a future, to rise from their graves and live again. The dead in the desert may represent the Jews of Odessa, who, during Bialik's life, were the victims of brutal pogroms. Bialik entreats the "dead" nation to arise and return home, suggesting that even when it seems that they are buried beneath the desert sands, life can begin again, against all odds and logic.

The *haftara* of *Parashat Vayera,* II Kings 4:8–38,[1] describes the birth and then rebirth of a child through the words of the prophet Elisha. What is the purpose of the story? It is not new or unique. Is it recounted in order to prove the greatness of the prophet, to show that he can perform miracles like Elijah before him? Perhaps it contains a more meaningful lesson about mankind's responsibility in this world.

Hospitality

Elisha travels from city to city in order to bring the word of God to the people. One of the cities he passes through regularly is the city of Shunem.[2] There he meets a woman who encourages him to eat in her home, and then conceives of the notion to build a room for the prophet.

This woman is described as an *isha gedola,* understood by many to mean a prominent woman, a description that does not appear elsewhere in Tanakh. This term could be a comment on her wealth, indicating that she owns fields and servants. Rashi views the phrase as a description of her importance,[3] connecting her to Avishag the Shunamite.[4] According to *Targum Yonatan,* the term reflects her spiritual status as a woman

1. Ashkenazic congregations read through verse 38, but Sephardic congregations end at verse 23.
2. Today this area is associated with the Arab village named Sula, located four kilometers east of Afula (in the portion of the tribe of Issachar; see Josh. 19:18). Some believe that the Shunamite woman's home is still standing and consider it an auspicious place to pray for children.
3. Rashi on II Kings 4:8.
4. Radak also cites this opinion, commenting on the fact that both women are referred to as Shunamites. Although there are about 125 years between the death of King David in 970 BCE (when Avishag took care of the aging king) and the ascent of Elisha in 845 BCE (when the story of the Shunamite woman takes place), the Midrash

with no sin. Malbim adds that her greatness stems from her righteous actions. The Midrash lists twenty-three righteous women, among them the Shunamite woman.[5] The Zohar goes as far as to state that this woman is greater than any woman who ever lived.[6] Accepting all of these descriptions, we can draw a composite picture of a woman who appreciates and recognizes greatness, performs acts of kindness, and has influence over her husband. She is the one who makes decisions in this house. Her life appears to be full. Our nameless woman is busy, involved in the community, and well known. She strives for spirituality, visiting the prophet regularly to learn from him (II Kings 4:23), and she is successful in her quest.

Why is she nameless? Many biblical women are anonymous. A woman with no name makes her more universal, and perhaps there were others like her. Maybe she is not so unusual.

Her husband, also nameless, appears to be quite passive. The Midrash[7] associates him with the prophet Iddo,[8] yet all of the interaction with Elisha is through his wife. Elisha never speaks to the husband, and although the Shunamite woman is careful to ask her husband's permission, he agrees with all the decisions she makes. He is obviously also involved in miracles, but he plays a passive role. We are left to wonder: Would Iddo the prophet have taken a back seat in all this? Could he have truly been the husband in this story?

Ralbag conjectures that since this story takes place in the early period of Elisha's years as a prophet, the extent of his prophetic abilities is not yet known. The Shunamite woman invites him in because she is hospitable – she invites everyone in. Her generosity of spirit applies to

---

says the two women are "sisters." This can be understood as a more general family connection.

5. *Otzar HaMidrashim* 23.
6. See the Zohar on Exodus 2:44, which states that most women resent guests, but not the Shunamite woman. She was unique in the joy that she took in hospitality and in her willingness to spend money on her guests.
7. *Pirkei DeRabbi Eliezer* 33.
8. Radak on I Kings 13:1 says Iddo was the "man of God" who was sent to Yerovoam, though that presents a time line problem, as the beginning of the period of the Kingdom of Judah around the year 925 BCE was eighty years before our story takes place.

all, not just the holy and famous. Subsequently, through her interactions with him,[9] she recognizes his godliness[10] and deems it appropriate to provide him with his own space.[11]

The Midrash on *Eshet Ḥayil*[12] associates the verse "She stretches out her palm to the poor" (Prov. 31:20) with the Shunamite woman because of the room she made for the prophet.[13] She and her husband want their visitor to be comfortable. The room they set aside is for both Elisha and his servant Gehazi,[14] and she furnishes it with a bed, table, chair, and lamp. These simple, common pieces of furniture also represent the Menora and the Table in the Temple.[15] With these references to the Temple, the Shunamite woman brings holiness into her home through her acts of kindness for a holy man of God.[16] We, too, have the potential to turn our homes into holy places like the Temple.[17] This is what we constantly strive for, to fulfill the verse "They shall make Me a Sanctuary and I will dwell in their midst" (Ex. 25:8).

For the second time in this passage, we see the term *vayehi hayom*, "one day." The Zohar states that whenever this term is used, it indicates that it is Rosh HaShana, the day that God judges the world.[18] It is for this reason that the prophet asks, "Shall I speak to the king on

9. It states in Berakhot 10b that women are better judges of guests.
10. Berakhot 10b also discusses a difference of opinion between Rav and Shmuel. One says that she never saw an (impure) fly near his table, and the other says that she never found emissions on his bedsheets.
11. *Metzudat David* on II Kings 4:10.
12. *Midrash Mishlei* (Buber) 31.
13. In Berakhot 10b, Rav and Shmuel differ as to what this room looked like. One says it was a roofless room that they closed in for the prophet. The other says it was a large room that was portioned off. The Gemara adds that the description in the verse refers to the quality of the room.
14. See II Kings 4:13, where Elisha says to the Shunamite woman, "You have shown us so much concern."
15. Sforno on Exodus 25:23.
16. *Reishit Ḥokhma, Shaar HaAnava,* chapter 3.
17. These objects may also be connected with the three commandments bestowed upon women: tithing *ḥalla*, lighting Shabbat candles, and observing the laws of family purity. These three elements are also found in Sarah's tent. See Rashi on Genesis 24:67 and *Sefer HaLikkutim* on Judges 15.
18. Zohar 3:231.

your behalf?" Elisha is asking whether he should speak to the King of the Universe, specifically on this day when all of mankind is judged.[19] The Shunamite woman replies, "I live among my own people," meaning: "Don't single me out on Rosh HaShana. I want to be viewed as part of the congregation."[20] She wishes to be judged as a member of the community. It is neither appropriate nor wise to be singled out, for the compassion of the blessed Holy One rests upon the entire people as one. She states that she has no personal request; her concern is for the community. When the prophet asks what she needs, the Shunamite woman replies that none of her neighbors are bothering her and, if necessary, her family will intervene on her behalf.[21] She may also be hinting that she views herself as a simple person who does not want to be paid back for the kindness that she performed.

The Miracle

From the Shunamite woman's answer, we are given the impression that everything is fine. She is content with her life and has no requests or needs; she feels that nothing is lacking. Everyone seems to be happy until Gehazi points out to Elisha that all is not perfect because there is no child. Without a child, there is no happiness and no continuity (Nedarim 64b). The Shunamite woman is surely aware of the situation, but she doesn't even think to ask for help in resolving it. Either it is too extraordinary a request, or she has learned to accept her lot in life and doesn't cry for what she doesn't have.[22]

It is interesting that it is Gehazi who notes the lack of a child. Did the prophet not realize? Either way, Elisha prophesies that his hostess will be rewarded with the miracle of a child. Nowhere else in Tanakh do we see a miracle of this magnitude initiated by a human. All other such incidents are a fulfillment of God's decree: For example, God promises via an angel that Sarah will have a child (Gen. 18:10); Eli says to Hannah,

---

19. Ibid. 2:44.
20. Ibid., *Beshalaḥ* 2:44b.
21. Radak on II Kings 4:13.
22. See "Barrenness" in this chapter (below) for another explanation.

"May the God of Israel grant what you seek of Him" (I Sam. 1:17); and an angel tells Samson's mother that she will have a child. In this case, though, it is Gehazi's idea. God's name is not even mentioned.

Why does Elisha go along with it? It would seem that once Gehazi suggests it, Elisha can't say no; it would be a sign of weakness or impotence. And why does God "go along" with the prophet? This is an important example of the teaching that "a righteous person decrees, and God fulfills the decree."[23] This reflects the greatness of Elisha,[24] and perhaps the woman did deserve a reward for her actions. The Midrash states that the fulfillment of Elisha's decree is an example of the precept "The will of those who fear Him He will do" (Ps. 145:19).[25]

The Shunamite woman reacts hesitantly. She has made a life for herself without children and seemingly accepts her fate. She is now filled with doubt – why open a can of worms? She is an *isha gedola,* a great woman, her days filled with acts of kindness. She doesn't know whether to laugh or cry at this news. She would certainly like to have a son, but she is cautious. She is also modest and shuns attention. She doubts whether she is worthy of being the recipient of such a great miracle, and she questions whether the prophet can indeed produce a miracle of this magnitude.[26]

Barrenness

The Shunamite woman is never actually called barren, unlike the other biblical women who are explicitly described as such. How is she different? She did have a child – but he has been killed.[27] She is not barren, just childless at this point. She has made peace with her situation.

Uriel Simon suggests that her barrenness is omitted lest we get the wrong impression and think that there is an ulterior motive behind

23. Job 22:28 expresses the same concept.
24. If God fulfills his decree, Elisha must be considered righteous.
25. *Pirkei DeRabbi Eliezer* 33.
26. Rashi on II Kings 4:16.
27. According to *Pirkei DeRabbi Eliezer* 32, her child was the prophet Iddo. However, the time line assumed for that explanation doesn't match up with the fact that Iddo did not live in Elisha's time.

her hospitality. If we know that the Shunamite woman is struggling with this challenge, we might question her sincerity in inviting a miracle worker into her home.[28]

Here we come to an interesting discussion: Is the Shunamite woman's acceptance of her childlessness something to be admired? Rabbi Elchanan Samet suggests that in fact, acceptance is the wrong response.[29] Why doesn't she give her husband a second wife? Why does she not turn to God and pray? Other childless women seek salvation from their suffering. In accepting her fate, it may be that rather than face reality, she ignores it or hides from it. When we compare her to the other barren women, she falls short. Rabbi Mordechai Sabato, however, believes otherwise.[30] He argues that the Shunamite woman's attitude is admirable, as one must accept their reality and not live with false expectations. As we have pointed out, the Shunamite woman is not bitter, and she creates a rich and fulfilling life for herself. She involves herself in helping others and communal matters, and hosts the prophet in her home. According to this view, she does face reality – and rather than focus on what she is lacking, she makes the most of it.[31] The question of how much a person should fight to change a situation is universal and timeless. How hard do we push, and when is it time to accept the reality and move forward?

As promised by the prophet, the Shunamite woman is rewarded with a son.

Death

Following this happy event, complications arise that force the Shunamite woman to question God's justice.

---

28. Rabbi Elchanan Samet, *Pirkei Elisha* [Hebrew] (Yedioth Books, 2009).
29. Rabbi Elchanan Samet, "*Elisha VeHaShunamit*," available at: https://www.etzion.org.il/he/tanakh/neviim/sefer-melakhim-bet/5-אלישע-והשונמית.
30. Rabbi Mordechai Sabato, "*Sipur HaShunamit*," in *Alei Etzion* 7, available at: http://www.haretzion.org/torah/yeshiva-publications/154-alei-etzion.
31. It strikes this author as somewhat strange that two men are analyzing how a woman dealt with her barrenness.

The story continues after an unspecified period of time. The child is old enough to go out to the field but not old enough to help, and he can still be held in the arms of a parent. While out in the field watching the harvest, the boy becomes deathly ill. Based on a simple reading of the text, the child dies of heatstroke. But the story demands a deeper understanding of the situation. Rabbi Samet sees this episode as an example of a pattern typical of the early prophets.[32] If there is a punishment, then there must have been a sin; therefore, the child's death must be a punishment for a sin. Who sinned, and what was the sin? Perhaps the Shunamite woman falls short in her child-rearing compared to the other barren women of the Bible.[33] All of their sons, including Isaac, Jacob, Joseph, Samson, and Samuel, to name a few, grow up to be prominent men who make major contributions to society. Other sources describe these sons growing up with greatness and becoming leaders, while in contrast the Shunamite woman's child simply plays in the field; he doesn't fit the same miraculous persona. Perhaps this is his mother's sin. Rabbi Samet suggests that the miraculous nature of the child's birth should have changed the Shunamite woman; now more is demanded of her. But she fails in this, and the child remains anonymous. He too has no name. The only thing we see the child doing every day is going out to the field, where he grows up – rather like Esau. Why isn't he learning Torah? The banality of his death by sunstroke underscores his passive, unexciting life.

On top of that, where is the happiness and celebration when he is born? Other barren women celebrate with praise, songs, parties – some acknowledgment of the miracle.[34] The Shunamite woman's sin may be found first in her lack of gratitude and then in not living up to expectations.

32. Rabbi Elchanan Samet, "*Elisha VeHaShunamit*," available at: https://www.etzion.org.il/he/tanakh/neviim/sefer-melakhim-bet/5-אלישע-והשונמית.

33. See, for example, these verses describing the children of other previously barren women: Genesis 25:27 (Jacob and Esau); Judges 13:24–25 (Samson); and I Samuel 2:21 (Samuel).

34. See Genesis 21:7–8 (Sarah); Genesis 30:33–34 (Rachel); and I Samuel 2:1 (Hannah).

Rabbi Samet quotes Rabbi Joseph B. Soloveitchik in *Kol Dodi Dofek*:

> Judaism states that the kindnesses of God are not given to man as an unconditional gift, without obligation; they require something in return; their essence imposes a moral, halakhic demand upon the man who enjoys them. Indeed, while loving-kindness emanates from the open, overflowing, generous hand of the Holy one, it is not an unlimited or unconditional gift. Such a gift is not absolute. The bestowing of good is always conditional and temporary. When God bestows wealth, property, influence, and honor, the recipient must know how to employ them; how to turn these precious gifts into fruitful, creative powers, how to include others in his happiness and greatness, and how to render loving-kindness with the divine kindnesses that emanate and issue forth to him from a never-ending front. If an abundance of good does not bring man to absolute subordination to the Holy one, then he is guilty of a fundamental sin resulting in the severe distress that in turn reminds him of his obligation to the Creator of the universe for the gift of His kindness.[35]

People who receive miracles have a certain responsibility. Miracles don't cost God anything, but He doesn't give out gifts. God gives on condition. Man has to give back in some way. Whether man is given wealth, intelligence, or honor, he must learn how to use the gifts that God gives. If he does not give to others, he is reneging on his responsibility to God.

Rabbi Soloveitchik continues:

> If God's grace, which is given to either an individual or a community, requires certain actions of the beneficiary, even if the gifts (such as wealth, honor, influence, power, etc., which are attained by exhausting efforts) are granted to man by natural means, how much more so is it true that Divine gifts given supernaturally in

35. Rabbi Joseph B. Soloveitchik, *Kol Dodi Dofek: Listen—My Beloved Knocks*, trans. David Gordon, 10.

> the form of miracles that transcend the framework of the elementary laws of historical causality must subject the recipient of the miracles to God. Miraculous grace places upon man an absolute responsibility to fulfill the larger imperative that calls out from the miracle. A transcendental imperative always accompanies activity.... Woe unto the beneficiary of a miracle who does not recognize it for what it is, and whose ear is deaf to the echo of the imperative that arises out of this metahistorical event.[36]

According to this view, the child dies because there is no appreciation for the miracle, no joy, and more importantly, because the Shunamite woman fails in her responsibility to raise the child in the appropriate manner. But what motivated her to act this way? Is this the way of an *isha gedola*, a great woman? Why doesn't she respond in the same way as Sarah and Hannah? Perhaps the answer is found in her status. We know that she is wealthy, the owner of fields and vineyards, that she has an active life, that her home is open to visiting dignitaries, and that she fills her time with meaningful, spiritual activities. The lack of a child does not demand of her a new relationship with God. It does not cause her to cry out in prayer, nor does she send her husband to pray on her behalf. When Elisha inquires as to what she needs, she replies that she wants for nothing. She does not feel a lack, and that is why her response is hesitant. Since she does not long for a child, it is hard for her to fully appreciate the miracle.

Rabbi David Sabato vehemently disagrees.[37] He asserts that the Shunamite woman is blameless, and the guilty party is in fact the prophet, Elisha. For the first time in history, a prophet takes it upon himself to grant a son to a childless couple. The woman does no wrong. She behaves with kindness and dignity, and does not even ask for the child. Why would God give her a child and then take it away? Why does the child die? Because of the prophet. The Gemara tells us there are three "keys"

36. Ibid., 23.
37. Rabbi David Sabato, "*Hemshekh Sippur HaIsha HaShunamit*," available at https://www.ybm.org.il/lesson?lesson=4324&format=V.

in God's treasure house, all connected to giving life.[38] Elisha "grabs" a key without asking for permission, without even praying about it, and in doing so oversteps his authority.

There is a vital element lacking in Elisha's blessing, so God teaches him a lesson. When Rachel asks Jacob for a child, he counters, "Am I in place of God?" (Gen. 30:2). When Hannah is blessed by Eli, he tells her that God will fulfill her request (I Sam. 1:17). Elisha, however, puts himself in place of God. As a result, there is a fault with his blessing and it expires. It is almost as if the child is guaranteed to die, because what comes from man can only be temporary in nature. There is a limit to the prophet's power, and the lesson is clear: be careful with what you "force" God to do. The child dies as a punishment for Elisha, and upon his death the prophet admits to not having understood that (II Kings 4:27). God wants to teach him a lesson in humble pie.[39]

Rabbi Samet also finds fault with Elisha for performing this miracle, noting that as he was no stranger to this home, he should have consulted with the woman before giving her this blessing, and he should have prepared her for this special child. The responsibility lies with the prophet. He should have been involved in educating and raising the child; perhaps then the child would have reached his potential.

The Shunamite woman, however, refuses to accept the prophet's failure. In her worldview, the prophet cannot fail. He only comes to help her: this is his responsibility, and he has the capability to fix the situation. She hadn't wanted the miracle to begin with. How can it be that God allows a miracle of this magnitude to be realized, only for it to end in death? She doesn't cry, nor is she overcome with grief. She has a deep-rooted belief in the justice of God and in His servant. The desecration of God's name which is a natural result of the child's death is intolerable for the Shunamite woman. If she wasn't fully cognizant of the miracle beforehand, now that the child is dead, she begins to realize the magnitude of the miracle and of what she has lost. Before the

38. Deuteronomy Rabba 7 and Taanit 2a state that God has three keys: the key of rain, the key of giving birth, and the key of the resurrection of the dead.

39. See Deuteronomy Rabba 8, which says that God allows the righteous to be like Him, but only to a certain extent.

child's birth, she had made peace with her childlessness, but this loss is not something that she is willing to accept.

Action

In Genesis, when Sarah hears about the death of her son, she has a heart attack and dies.[40] The Shunamite woman reacts differently, immediately taking action and beginning her repentance; there is no mourning or crying, only concrete problem-solving. She places the dead child on the prophet's bed and informs her husband that she has to make an immediate trip to Elisha. She saddles her own donkey. Upon reaching the prophet, a trip of about twenty kilometers – a five-hour journey – she throws herself at his feet. This behavior is quite different from the reserved interaction she had with him in her home. The Shunamite woman addresses him harshly and refuses to leave. The miracle itself does not induce a response from her, but the tragedy does. The suffering now motivates her to take decisive action. She is both determined and filled with trust in God.

Rabbi Samet quotes Rabbi Soloveitchik:

> Just as God obliges man to perform deeds of a higher order and demands creative and innovative actions from the individual or the populace, so does suffering require the repair of the soul and the cleansing of life – if at the time of God's favor and beneficence one was not aroused to action. For it happens that man is summoned to repair, through his afflictions, the damage he caused in God's creation at the hour when the Holy One extended His bounty. The feeling of subordination to the Almighty and the understanding of one's obligation to purify and sanctify one's self by dint of one's suffering must brighten man's soul when he finds himself in distress and perplexed by his existence.[41]

---

40. Rashi on Genesis 23:2.
41. Rabbi Joseph B. Soloveitchik, *Kol Dodi Dofek: Listen – My Beloved Knocks*, trans. David Gordon, 10.

He explains that just as one should react to the good that we experience from God, the bad, too, demands reaction. The suffering is the last warning, forcing man to react. God is calling out to man and he must not miss this opportunity.

Just as good things demand a response, so does tragedy. If good does not motivate people to react, sometimes it is the bad that forces the reaction. Suffering awakens an awareness of what is now lacking. Suddenly, the Shunamite woman appreciates what she had and is aware of the tremendous miracle that was, but now it is too late.

The Shunamite woman doesn't tell her husband about the child's death. She doesn't even want to say it. Verbalizing something is a way of saying that it's true,[42] and she doesn't want the burial preparations to begin. She knows that miracles need to be done very privately.[43] If everyone knows that he is dead, she cannot expect a revival. So she hides the body in the special room that she prepared for the prophet. She trusts that the holiness of the prophet will prevent the decomposition of the body in the summer heat. In addition, she is relying on the responsibility and ability of the prophet to take control of the situation that he set in motion.

The Shunamite woman makes an excuse for why she unexpectedly needs go to the prophet, as it is not Rosh Ḥodesh or Shabbat.

According to Sephardic tradition, the *haftara* ends at this point. This is not surprising when we realize that the Shunamite woman has passed her test. She deeply believes in the messenger of God, concluding that God gave the prophet the ability to give her a child, and so God can also give the prophet the ability to bring him back to life.[44] She believes that God defied nature to bring this child into existence and there is no reason He can't do it again.

---

42. Ralbag on II Kings 12:18.
43. *Metzudat David* on II Kings 4:23.
44. This complete confidence in the possibility of God's miracles is also seen in Taanit 25a, where the story is told of the daughter of R. Ḥanina b. Tradyon, who lights vinegar instead of oil on Erev Shabbat. R. Ḥanina tells her not to worry: just as God performs the "miracle" of causing oil to burn, He can cause vinegar to burn.

At the Prophet's Feet

Elisha sees the Shunamite woman approaching and sends Gehazi out to greet her and ask if all is well. She approaches the prophet and throws herself at his feet. Gehazi, completely misreading the situation, tries to push her away. Perhaps he suspects something is amiss and recalls whose idea the child was in the first place. Elisha, being more perceptive, commands Gehazi to leave her alone. He understands that something has occurred.

Radak points out that it does not behoove the woman or the prophet for her to grovel.[45] At the beginning of the story, she is careful to maintain a respectful distance between them. While Gehazi communicates with her, she stands back (II Kings 4:15).

Now Elisha admits that he does not know why she has come. There is an inconsistency between his ability to perform great miracles and his human limitations. This is the first time he mentions God's name in the story, saying, "The Lord has hidden this from me and did not tell me" (II Kings 4:27), and the first time he shows humility, as he acknowledges that he is limited and incompetent without God's help.

Reaction

The Shunamite woman then begins her desperate plea: "Did I ask my lord for a son?" (II Kings 4:28). She hints that the issue lies with the prophet, reminding Elisha that he is responsible for bringing this child to earth. Apparently, this was something that she has been afraid of from the beginning, which helps us to understand her hesitant reaction to the prophet's promise.[46] Elisha sends Gehazi ahead with his staff and a series of strict instructions: go quickly, no stopping, don't talk to people, don't be distracted, and don't waste any time. In this way, the prophet admits his responsibility and shows that he believes it is within his power to help. But the fact that he doesn't immediately accompany them suggests that he doesn't realize just how dire the situation really is.

---

45. Radak on II Kings 4:27.
46. Rashi on II Kings 4:16.

Perhaps he thinks the boy is very sick and doesn't understand that he is actually dead. Maybe he wants to minimize the necessity of the miracle by making it seem that even his servant could perform it.

Gehazi, of course, is unsuccessful in his mission. Gehazi doesn't follow the rules; he was told not to tell and he tells (II Kings 4:29). Miracles are private affairs and not for public consumption. Gehazi is a denier of the resurrection of the dead (Sanhedrin 90a), and Radak says he spoke of his mission in order to mock it, questioning the staff's ability to revive the child.[47] He is simply unworthy of performing a miracle.[48]

But it is not fair to blame Gehazi in this chapter, as his greed is only exposed later (II Kings 5). Gehazi's lack of success may be tied to Elisha's shortcomings. Why does Elisha have to try twice to revive the child? God wants to teach Elisha a lesson. This is something he needs to do himself. Gehazi is unsuccessful because Elisha has not yet repented.

The Shunamite woman demands that Elisha come with her; she is not willing to accept Gehazi and the staff as a replacement for the prophet. Earlier in the chapter, she needed nothing from the prophet, but now she demands his help. Here she is finally described as "the boy's mother" (II Kings 4:30), fighting for the child and her motherhood.

Elisha arrives at the woman's home after a long and tiring journey, enters the room, and closes the door. He does this so that he can focus on his prayer, and also so that no one will witness what he is about to do.[49] Miracles work better when they are hidden from the public eye.[50]

Repentance

Elisha performs mouth-to-mouth resuscitation, giving of himself to the child.[51] It is a form of giving birth a second time, this time with proper preparation, prayer, and taking responsibility. He humbles himself with his prayer and acknowledges God's role in this situation.

47. Radak on II Kings 4:29.
48. Ralbag on II Kings 4:29.
49. Ibid.
50. In a separate incident at the beginning of the chapter (verse 4), Elisha tells a widow to close the door in anticipation of a miracle that is about to happen.
51. Radak on II Kings 4:34.

Verse 35 describes Elisha pacing back and forth. Ralbag[52] and Radak[53] insist that this must be more prayer, his heart concentrating through his physical actions. The child is revived. Elisha calls to the child's mother and tells her to lift him up. The Shunamite woman again falls on the prophet's feet, humbling herself. In her earlier desperation, she was demanding, but now she returns to her position as a humble servant. Thereafter, she leaves the scene wordlessly.

With this simple act of prostration, the Shunamite woman repents. In doing so, she acknowledges that the events that have taken place are outside of nature. It is also a way of thanking the prophet. At the end of the story, she finally shows appreciation. From a tale of childlessness and miracles comes a powerful story of repentance. If the Shunamite woman did not react properly to the miracle of the child's birth, she corrects her actions upon his death. She now appreciates the miracle and refuses to accept that it could expire. Whereas earlier, she hesitated to accept his promise, now she throws herself at the feet of the prophet, acknowledging her belief. Elisha, too, undergoes a growth process. At the beginning of the story, he takes too much credit for himself, but he learns. He admits that he doesn't know why the Shunamite woman is seeking him out, as God didn't tell him. When he arrives to revive the child, we see him praying – he is again in a situation where he needs to take one of God's "keys," but this time he asks permission. We later see Elisha taking responsibility for the child when he warns them of the impending famine and tells them to move.

Finally, the child is no longer anonymous. On the contrary, he is someone famous:[54] Habakkuk, so called because of the Hebrew word *ḥibbuk*, "hug,"[55] as this child is hugged twice by his mother, once when he is born and once when he is reborn. Alternatively, the name could represent the fact that the child is hugged once by his mother and once by

52. Ralbag on II Kings 4:35.
53. Radak on II Kings 4:35.
54. The Zohar 1:7 notes that the book of Habakkuk gives us no personal information about the prophet, not even a mention of the king's life during which he prophesied. There are many different opinions as to when Habakkuk lived. Appropriately, one of the themes of the book is why bad things happen to good people.
55. See II Kings 4:16.

the prophet. The Sages also associate the revived child with the prophet Habakkuk because it is inconceivable that a person who had two such miracles occur to him would not achieve greatness.

The prophet commands the woman to raise up the child (II Kings 4:36), meaning raise him spiritually to the position in which he belongs. This is the emotion that was lacking at the beginning of the story. This concludes the full repentance of both the Shunamite woman and the prophet. Indeed, in the epilogue to this story (in chapter 8), we see the prophet taking responsibility for the family. He is now involved in their lives in the way that he should have been from the very beginning.

The Connection Between the *Parasha* and the *Haftara*

The two stories bear some striking similarities. First, both women are childless, and after inviting guests into their respective homes, they are told with the same expression – *ka'et ḥaya,* "this time next year"[56] – that they will each have a son. Both women respond with skepticism.[57] Both have elderly husbands, and this fact is stated once and then not repeated.[58] As promised, the sons are born.[59] Both sons come very close to death and experience some sort of revival.[60]

However, while the similarities are pronounced, there are also some important differences. As pointed out earlier, in Sarah's case, the child is promised by God. In the story of the Shunamite woman, it is Elisha's idea first, and all the troubles stem from there. Another difference is found in Abraham's response when he is told by God to go and sacrifice his son – he accepts the command and does not question it. The Shunamite woman, however, does not accept the position that God has placed her in when her child falls ill. She fights for her child's life.

We also find similarities between the story of the Shunamite woman and the story of Hannah. God "remembers" them both on Rosh

56. These are the only two times in the Bible that this expression appears.
57. Sarah laughs, and the Shunamite woman pleads, "Do not delude your servant."
58. God doesn't repeat it to Abraham, and Elisha does not repeat to the Shunamite woman what Gehazi has said.
59. See Genesis 21:2 (Sarah) and II Kings 4:17 (Shunamite woman).
60. *Pirkei DeRabbi Eliezer* 31.

HaShana, and the term *vayehi hayom*, "one day," appears in both stories. Both women are barren, and at some point, both women's behavior is judged as inappropriate.[61] Both Hannah and the Shunamite woman are described as *marat nefesh*, "wretched." Both have husbands who are secondary characters, supporting their wives and allowing them to make their own decisions and determine their own actions. Yet both these women seem to be lacking a partner. Hannah's husband does not understand the depth of her suffering and she is forced to pray alone. The Shunamite woman hides the child's death from her husband and travels to the prophet alone.

For many years, the Land of Israel, as well as its children, seemed to be dead. Yet miraculously, Israel now breathes and even flourishes among the nations of the world. Once we have experienced this miracle, we cannot take it for granted. We must appreciate it, and when necessary, we must fight for its survival. As Ezekiel prophesied:

> So, prophesy; say to them: So says the Lord God: See, I am opening up your graves; I will lift you out of your graves, My people, and I will bring you to the soil of Israel. You will know that I am the Lord when I open up your graves, when I lift you out of your graves, My people. I will put My breath into you, and you will come to life; I will set you upon your soil, and you will know that I am the Lord; I have spoken, and I will do it, declares the Lord.[62]

---

61. Eli thinks Hannah is drunk, and Gehazi pushes the Shunamite woman away from the prophet.
62. Ezekiel 37:12–14.

Part Two

Barren Women Who Never Bear Children

לא היה לה ילד עד יום מותה

(II Samuel 6:23)

Chapter 5

Jephthah's Daughter

Legends of child sacrifice figure prominently in Greek mythology. In one famous tale, we meet the Cretan king and military commander Idomeneus, who promises Poseidon, the god of the sea and storms, that he will sacrifice the first person who greets him upon his safe return home from his stormy sea voyage. The king's son becomes the hapless, unwitting victim and is sacrificed when he is the first to greet his returning father. This is the version of the story that is ascribed to Apollodorus of the second century.[1]

In another story, a play written by Euripides in 406 BCE, Agamemnon is the leader of the Greek troops on their way to vanquish Troy. To appease the angry gods who objected to the slaughter of a sacred deer, he promises to sacrifice his daughter, Iphigenia. There are different versions of the myth. In some, she is sacrificed, while in others she is saved by the goddess Artemis.

These are but two examples among many. We do not know whether the book of Judges was known to the Greek authors, though because Judges predates Euripides by about five hundred years, it is possible, at least in theory. What is clear, however, is that child sacrifice

1. In the third book of *The Odyssey*, Idomeneus returns home safely with no promises of sacrifices.

was a well-known practice in the ancient world as a tribute or a means of appeasing angry gods.

The Story of Jephthah's Daughter

Judges 11 relates the tragic story of Jephthah the Gileadite, the tenth judge of Israel who lived in the eleventh century BCE. There have been forty-five years of peace and tranquility under the previous two judges, Tola son of Puah and Jair the Gileadite. Following Jair's demise, the people revert to the sin that pollutes the entire book of Judges: idol worship. During this period the practice enters an entirely new dimension. Until now, the Israelites had believed in a synchronous religion, adding false gods to their worship of the true God. Now, however, they start to ignore the true God and exclusively worship the "power" and "authority" of idolatry (Judges 10:6).

As punishment, God subjugates the Israelites under the Philistines and Ammonites, who oppress them with continuous harassment (Judges 10:7–9). The nation's attempts at repentance are rebuffed as God declares that He will not tolerate their sinning only to have them sheepishly return to His embrace when they are faced with the consequences of their wayward conduct (Judges 10:11–14). The Israelites attempt to demonstrate their undivided devotion to God by destroying all their idols (Judges 10:16)[2] as the Ammonites amass at the border, threatening imminent attack. The heads of the Gileadite region realize the need to find a qualified military leader for the inevitable battle (Judges 10:17–18).

God provides the generation with the leader who is appropriate for their diminished spiritual level. The military elite appeal to Jephthah to lead the campaign. Jephthah is introduced as the son of the Gileadite clan's leader and a woman described as a *zona,* a harlot (Judges 11:1).[3] We learn that Jephthah has been banished by his vindictive half-brothers. Why does his father allow this humiliation? Jephthah's pedigree (or lack thereof) is relevant in order to understand why he has been expelled

2. Rashi says that God rejects their repentance, but Radak believes that He accepts it.
3. Radak says that Jephthah's mother was a concubine, *Targum Yonatan* turns her into an innkeeper, and Ralbag says that she was just from a different tribe.

from his family. The brothers don't want to share their inheritance with a brother of dubious heritage (Judges 11:2), a son from the wrong mother.[4]

In ancient times, a cast-off with no land faced almost insurmountable obstacles, and predictably, Jephthah joins a hoodlum gang. He settles in the land of Tov, where he becomes the chief ruffian (Judges 11:3). Ironically, these social misfits live in the eponymous "good" land. They likely survive by thievery and violence, and Jephthah must have had the charisma, strength, fortitude, and intelligence to lead this group.

When the heads of the Gileadite tribe ask him to lead the army, Jephthah takes offense and accuses them of insincerity and tending to their own self-interests (Judges 11:7). *Daat Mikra* suggests that they were trying to hire Jephthah's whole gang as mercenaries to fight in their place.[5] The Israelites are in desperate straits – the enemy has already set up launch positions at the border in a prelude to armed conflict – but Jephthah isn't willing to budge. The statesmen up the ante and extend their offer to include political leadership. Jephthah, craving validation and acknowledgment, cedes to the request and is appointed the head of state. The entire scenario is sweet revenge for Jephthah, as it forces the leaders to admit their arrogance and come groveling for help.

The flawed Jephthah, imbued with a healthy measure of hubris, is nonetheless the first to acknowledge the need for divine intervention in order to triumph over the formidable enemy. During the negotiations he is the first to mention the need for God's help to achieve victory (Judges 11:9), and indeed the spirit of the Lord descends upon him (Judges 11:29).

Meeting the Enemy

Jephthah begins with diplomacy in an honest effort to stave off the inevitable horrors of war. He negotiates with the king of Ammon as an equal and presents intelligent arguments. He explains that the Israelites did not steal land from the Ammonites; rather they inherited the land three hundred years earlier during the time of Moses, when their ancestors battled Sihon and Og (Judges 11:15–21). The Israelites did not initiate the war, and God was on their side. The valid arguments in Jephthah's

4. Jephthah's story echoes those of Ishmael and Joseph.
5. Y. Elitzur, *Daat Mikra* on Judges [Hebrew] (Mossad HaRav Kook), 118.

monologue cast him as an experienced, smart, and talented leader who is familiar with Jewish history.

Jephthah attacks the Ammonites from the rear flank, taking them completely by surprise. This tactic is fraught with extreme risk. If the enemy repels the surprise offensive, the attackers are trapped behind enemy lines in hostile territory, not to mention the danger of the strategy being leaked to the wary foe. Jephthah elects to take a huge gamble, and the nation prevails. However, he ultimately loses because his victory means the death of his daughter.

The Vow

Before the battle, Jephthah makes a fatal vow to God. He promises that if he is successful in battle, then whoever (or whatever) first crosses the threshold of his house to greet him will be consecrated as a sacrifice to God. Upon his return, it is his only daughter, sometimes referred to as Tanot (Judges 11:40), who rushes out to greet him, thus becoming the tragic victim of his ill-conceived oath.

At the war's end and safe return of the forces, where were the people? Where were the leaders who appointed him? From a broader perspective, the context surrounding the vow is striking. The narrative omits any mention of celebratory masses lining the streets to greet Jephthah and his troops upon their triumphant return from the battlefield.[6] No Canyon of Heroes–style thoroughfare s filled with adoring and thankful crowds showering victorious soldiers with hosannas or joyous dancing and singing awaited these battle-weary troops. Even though Jephthah is their designated leader and savior, apparently, the populace never respects him. He is still viewed as a shadowy, underworld warlord who is best avoided. He expects a full-blown victory parade, but only his daughter shows up.

In I Samuel, King Saul similarly takes a vow which would have led to the death of his son, Jonathan – if not for the people interceding, refusing to allow Saul to fulfill the vow (I Sam. 14:24). Why doesn't this happen in Jephthah's time? Why is there no public outcry to save his daughter?

---

6. Compare to I Samuel 18:7.

Let us take a step back. What is Jephthah thinking when he makes his vow? Perhaps he expects to see an animal suitable for sacrifice coming out of his house. But did animals live in people's homes? And if his intention was animal sacrifice, what prevented him from clearly specifying that? Traditionally, women would greet returning warriors, as we see in I Samuel 18:6, where the women come *likrat*, "to meet" King Saul to celebrate his victory. The verb *likrat* refers exclusively to people. Jephthah also uses the term *likrat* in his vow, so it is likely that he is indeed referring to the greeting party that he expects to see upon his return, rather than a sacrificial animal. And so the question stands: Was Jephthah contemplating offering human sacrifices?

In my view, the purpose of Jephthah's vow is pseudo-humility. When he realizes that the expected reception is going to be underwhelming, he pretends that he is willing to forgo the accolades and adulation that come with being the war hero. With this vow, the Gileadean strongman feigns humility while actually demonstrating his arrogance. Jephthah's aim is for the people to hear about the outrageous vow and stay home. He will appear righteous and pious in the eyes of onlookers without having to perform any real act of piety. To show his generosity, he doesn't limit his gift to a specific number of sacrificial animals. In the same way that Abraham negotiated his transaction when purchasing the burial plot of Makhpela from Efron (Gen. 23), Jephthah leaves the amount open-ended.

According to the Midrash, there are four vows made in Tanakh.[7] Two have positive outcomes: the Israelites are victorious in battle[8] and Hannah commits to consigning her son to Temple duty, should God bless her with a child (I Sam. 1). By contrast, the other two vows have tragic results: Rachel dies prematurely, causing Jacob great suffering,[9] and Jephthah loses his daughter.

7. *Yalkut Shimoni* on Judges 65.
8. See Numbers 28:20. In the time of Moses, they vow to consecrate the captured cities of Midian should they achieve success in the military campaign.
9. See Genesis 28:20–22. Upon his father-in-law's accusation that one of the fleeing members of Jacob's party has stolen his property, Jacob vows that the thief will be punished. Meanwhile, his wife Rachel has stolen and hidden the idol without his knowledge.

The Gemara (Taanit 4) lists three people who request help from God. Of these, Eliezer, servant of Abraham, who asks God to direct him to a suitable mate for Isaac, and Saul, king of Israel, are both given an affirmative response. But the third person, Jephthah, is not.[10] Why doesn't God save Jephthah from his own perilous words? The structure of the vows to which God responds positively are substantively different from that of Jephthah. The fulfillment of the other vows is directly related to those requests. Hannah cannot devote her son to a lifetime of Temple service if God doesn't grant her a son. The Israelites cannot donate the spoils of war unless they win the war. In the cases of the vows of Eliezer and Saul, the subject needs to display acts of kindness or bravery, so the clause is not arbitrary. Jephthah's vow, however, is not directly connected to his victory, and the clause is completely random. The Midrash asks, "What would he have done had a non-kosher animal walked out the door?"[11] Through the way God responds to each vow, He is sending a subtle message about the importance of being careful with one's words.[12]

Why Didn't Jephthah Annul the Vow?

Perhaps there are technical reasons for Jephthah's decision not to even attempt to annul his vow. Nahmanides suggests that wartime vows cannot be annulled (Lev. 27:29). It would seem that *a priori*, the vow is void because his commitment is not applicable. Yet this doesn't concern Jephthah, and after blaming his victim for coming out of the house, he rends his clothes in mourning (Judges 11:35).

This is Jephthah's tragic flaw. He makes a promise that he believes he cannot recant. In order to annul the vow, he would have to go to Phinehas the high priest. Jephthah feels that because he is the head of state, the priest should come to him, but the priest believes that Jephthah should be the one to come to him. Caught between the two

10. Other versions of this include the vow of Otniel ben Kenaz to give his daughter's hand in marriage to the man who would capture Kiryat Sefer.
11. Leviticus Rabba 37:4.
12. *Tanḥuma, Beḥukotai* 7.

egos is the unfortunate daughter who suffers a lifetime of consequences.[13] Jephthah's hubris does not allow him to seek help or admit to having made a mistake. He is acutely aware that if he annuls his promise, the Gileadean leaders might annul their own promise and remove him from his new position of leadership.

Some commentators contend that Jephthah is an ignoramus, and so he is unaware of the Torah law stating that vows can be annulled.[14] Others suggest that perhaps he thinks that a head of state cannot go back on his word.[15]

The Daughter's Reaction

Jephthah's daughter's willing acceptance of her fate is surprising. She declares that once a promise is made and God has upheld His side of the bargain, a person must fulfill their obligation (Judges 11:36). Her nobility shines through in her answer, which has no hint of self-pity or threats. She maintains a stoic acceptance of the circumstances.

Midrash Tanḥuma, however, envisions Jephthah's daughter fruitlessly arguing with him, citing precedents from others who have annulled their vows, such as Jacob, who did not relinquish a tenth of his children (Gen. 28:22).[16] In Judges 11:37, the daughter requests two months "to roam the *harim*" (translated as hills or mountains) and mourn her virginity. Radak [17]explains that the term *harim* is a reference to the Rabbinic High Court; she wants to appeal to the court to annul the vow. The court cannot help her, though, because the annulment request needs to come from Jephthah. While the text portrays the daughter as a passive victim who encourages her father to fulfill his promise, the Midrash ascribes to her intelligence, feeling, and courage in confronting her fearsome father Jephthah in an effort to change her destiny. She may have considered fleeing into the mountains, but this idea is rejected. In ancient times,

13. *Yalkut Shimoni* 68 and Genesis Rabba 60:3.
14. *Tanḥuma, Beḥukotai* 5.
15. Nahmanides on Leviticus 27:29.
16. *Tanḥuma, Beḥukotai* 5.
17. Judges 11:37.

disassociating oneself from one's home and family was highly dangerous for a man, and essentially impossible for a lone woman.

The Victim's Fate

We are not told exactly what becomes of Jephthah's daughter. The verse simply states: "He did to her what he had vowed to do" (Judges 11:39), leading to a dispute among the commentators. The prevalent view is that Jephthah indeed offered his daughter as a sacrifice (Taanit 4a). In doing so, the man who insisted on being a leader has destroyed any chance of a monarchic dynasty, as she is his only descendant (Judges 11:34). It is surprising that many commentators take this approach, given God's abhorrence of human sacrifice. If Jephthah had indeed offered his daughter as a sacrifice, one would expect severe condemnation in the text. Yet the text remains silent. This perspective is equally difficult to understand simply because child sacrifice is anathema to a religion that strongly values life and procreation.[18]

The text includes the point of the daughter and her friends crying over her virginity (Judges 11:38). This seems an unusual angle; surely, if she were about to be sacrificed, they would be mourning her impending death rather than her virginity. An interesting view is taken by commentators who lived in Christian Europe and were therefore familiar with the concept of a convent. They suggest that rather than sacrificing his daughter, Jephthah builds an isolated hut where she lives out her remaining years as a hermit.[19] According to this view, the daughter and her friends are grieving her loss of any chance of motherhood.

Either way, this young woman's life is ruined to preserve her father's dignity. Jephthah is a troubled, difficult character who is influenced by the environment in which he lives. After destroying his daughter's life, Jephthah feels threatened by the tribe of Ephraim and stages a civil war that leads to the deaths of thousands.[20]

---

18. See Deuteronomy 12:31.
19. Radak, Ralbag, Abrabanel, Malbim, and *Metzudat David* take this view.
20. See Judges 12.

It almost doesn't matter whether Jephthah's daughter is killed or lives a life of isolation. Either way, her life is wrecked by her father. She dies barren, leaving no progeny and no continuation.

Chapter 6

Batya

The term "righteous among the nations" is reserved for gentiles who risked their lives to save Jews during the Holocaust. In order to behave in a moral and honorable way, they endangered not only themselves but also their families and possessions. Furthermore, these acts were usually intentionally done without fanfare, far from the spotlight and with little chance of acclaim. These few courageous individuals refused to remain passive as unspeakable atrocities were being committed by those who viewed Jews as parasites.

In the poem titled "The Righteous of the World," Haim Hefer highlights the tremendous fortitude that these brave souls displayed by reversing the situation:

> I ask and ask, "Oh, my dear God,
> could I have done the same thing?"
>
> In a sea of hate stood my home,
> could I shelter a foreign son in my home?

The first "righteous among the nations" can actually be found millennia earlier – in ancient Egypt. At Pharaoh's behest, all baby boys delivered to Jewish mothers are to be thrown to their deaths in the Nile River.

Rabbi Yisrael Meir Lau points out that by choosing to save the females while murdering all the males, Pharaoh is the first to make a "selection."[1] Moses's mother places him in a basket in the reeds of the river, knowing that she cannot conceal her newborn indefinitely. Moses is then discovered by Batya,[2] the princess of Egypt, who rescues him and raises him as her own, ignoring legalities and brazenly defying her father (Ex. 2:3–5).

The story of Batya's insubordination follows the pattern of the midwives: women who refuse to perform the immoral act of infanticide. In the same way that the midwives defy the egregious decree of Pharaoh, Pharaoh's own rebellious daughter chooses to flout her father's outrageous diktat.

Batya's insubordination is most surprising given her position in the royal household. She is a member of Egypt's upper echelon, and yet she violates her father's decree.

When she sets out to save the baby, her maidservants voice their strong opposition.[3] Perhaps they are (rightfully) afraid of becoming involved in breaking the dictator's laws. Batya has been raised in a society that teaches its members to detest and fear the Israelites, a society that condones torture and genocide. As an esteemed member of the royal family, she has been endowed with everything, yet she courageously rejects her society's worldview. Who enlightens her, telling her that murdering Jews is unacceptable? How does she have the audacity to rebel against her upbringing? Even more astounding is the fact that not only does Batya save a Jewish child, she raises him in Pharaoh's palace! What makes her act with such temerity, as though one can publicly disrespect the king of the mighty Egyptian empire with no consequences?

---

1. See "Chief Rabbi Lau speaks on Holocaust Remembrance Day," available at: http://www.youtube.com/watch?v=f8KqIsk9rJc.
2. The more correct transliteration of her name may be Bitya.
3. See Exodus Rabba 1 and Sota 12b.

The Child's Name

Batya chooses the name Moses for the baby she rescues (Ex. 2:10). The Midrash teaches that Moses had at least ten names,[4] but God uses the name given by Batya exclusively so as to honor and reward her act of kindness in saving his life.[5] The name Moses comes from Batya's act of drawing him out of the water. It also reflects his greatest accomplishment: drawing the Jews out of Egypt.[6] Was Batya a prophetess (Sota 12b)? Did she speak Hebrew? Ibn Ezra contends that the name Moses is a translation from an ancient Egyptian word, as Batya did not speak Hebrew.[7] Still, one wonders whether she had reason to learn Hebrew. Perhaps she asked Jochebed, Moses's birth mother, for the translation?[8]

The River

Batya finds the baby at the river, but why is she there in the first place? Sforno points out that it is not befitting a princess to publicly bathe in the river.[9] We would expect that a person of her status would order her slaves to haul the water, heat it, and prepare a luxuriating bath. The Midrash addresses this question and suggests that Batya goes to the river to purify herself from her father's idols.[10] Rashi takes it a step further and suggests that she intends to immerse herself in the river as the final ritual of the conversion process.[11] While Rashi's explanation is appealing, it is difficult to justify, as there was no concept of conversion before the Jewish nation was forged at Mount Sinai with the giving of the Torah. What is reflected in Rashi's approach, however, is Batya's clear desire to sever her connection to her upbringing and surrounding society and throw her lot in with the oppressed slaves.

---

4. Leviticus Rabba 1.
5. Exodus Rabba 1.
6. *Kli Yakar* on Exodus 6:2.
7. Ibn Ezra on Exodus 2:10.
8. Abrabanel on Exodus 2:10.
9. Sforno on Exodus 2:5.
10. Exodus Rabba 23.
11. Rashi on Megilla 13a.

What would have prompted Rashi to offer this interpretation, which is seemingly unsupported by the simple reading of the text? It would appear that this explanation is quite logical when considering the context. Batya rebels against her father's decree in an utter rejection of the prevalent social hierarchy. The next step is a commitment to the oppressed population she identifies with, the enslaved Jews. We may also find an explanation for Rashi's suggestion from a careful reading of the text. The verse (Ex. 2:5) states that Batya goes *lirḥotz al hayeor,* "to bathe *on* the river." The correct version should read *lirḥotz bayeor,* "to bathe *in* the river." Rashi explains that she bathes "above the river," meaning on a higher spiritual plane, and in doing so, she also rejects the claim that the river is a deity, as the Egyptians believe.[12]

As Moses is born on the seventh day of Adar (Kiddushin 38a), and his mother hides him for three months before placing him in a basket in the river (Ex. 2:2), it follows that the date that Batya rescues Moses is the sixth of Sivan,[13] which corresponds with the date that the Jews received the Torah at Mount Sinai. The day of her personal conversion precisely foreshadows the nation of slave-refugees converting into an independent nation unified by an official religion. On the day she recognizes the true God, she saves the person who will eventually bring the entire nation to recognize the Almighty.

Some commentators suggest that rather than visit the river herself, Batya looks out from the palace onto the river, sees a basket, and sends her servant to retrieve it.[14] Others argue that it is a hot day, and she goes to avail herself of the river's cooling waters.[15] Still others propose that she goes down to the river because it is known for its health benefits, and she is seeking a cure for her familial skin disorder, leprosy.[16] In the Talmud, this disease is the physical manifestation of a spiritual disease, bringing us back to her need for some sort of cleansing (Arakhin 16a). In this view, as soon as she touches the basket, she is miraculously healed,[17]

12. Exodus Rabba 9:9.
13. Ibid. 1:24.
14. Sforno on Exodus 2:10.
15. *Targum Yonatan* on Exodus 2:10.
16. Exodus Rabba 1.
17. Ibid. 1:23.

leading her to the understanding that this child is unique, which inspires her to save him.

While the reason for Batya's presence at the river is hotly debated by the commentators, it is clear that her rebellious and courageous act of rescuing the Jewish baby belies an exceptional inner fortitude and moral compass. Her first act as a Jew is merciful and compassionate, both traits that are associated with the Jewish nation (Yevamot 79a) and qualities that she successfully helps Moses to develop.

The verse states that she sent *amata* to retrieve the basket (Ex. 2:5). The Sages define *amata* in two irreconcilable ways: R. Neḥemya says that she sends her servants,[18] while R. Yehuda claims that she extends her hand;[19] the basket is out of reach, but miraculously, her hand lengthens and she manages to grasp the floating basket.[20] Whether her hand stretches or a maid brings the basket to her, the message is clear: in order for God to help man, man has to take the initiative.[21] Even if one's goals appear to be out of reach – and even impossible – when a person makes a concerted effort to start the process, God helps us to succeed. Likewise, if man seeks redemption, God waits for him to make the first move.

Strength of Character

How does Batya know that the helpless baby in the floating basket is Jewish? Palace astrologers could not determine unequivocally if the putative savior was Jewish or Egyptian (since Moses was Jewish but raised as an Egyptian), so Pharaoh amended his decree to include even Egyptian babies.[22] Some suggest that Moses's circumcision[23] would have been an easy way for her to determine the infant's identity. More interestingly, others propose that she is sensitive enough to perceive that God's aura is with this child (Sota 12a). Is it plausible that she reaches

18. *Ama*, meaning a female servant, is the root of the word *amata*. See Exodus 21:7.
19. *Ama* is the term used for handbreadth, a measurement frequently found in the Torah (e.g., Genesis 6:15).
20. See Sota 12b and Exodus Rabba 1:23.
21. See Exodus 14:15.
22. Rashi on Exodus 1:22.
23. Rashbam on Exodus 2:6.

such an exalted level of spiritual heights that she is able to sense God's presence? It is clear that she appreciates ideals that her father and his society do not. She understands the value and sees the potential of each human, regardless of race, a radical idea in ancient times. This divine encounter is what convinces her that the rebellion against her father is morally correct.

How does Batya have the audacity to bring a baby into the palace, especially since it is clear that he is Jewish? A seamless approach to understanding this remarkable biblical figure is the assumption that she is childless.[24] This approach helps to resolve a number of issues. As the royal princess, it is entirely possible that Pharaoh has a special place in his heart for his barren daughter, and he is unable to refuse her request to add Moses to the royal household.[25] The Midrash describes how she would hold Moses and kiss him.[26] This is consistent with the theory that she does not have her own children to cherish and embrace and therefore directs her love toward her adopted son, Moses. It is reported that Batya refuses to take Moses outside because he is so beautiful, and even Pharaoh would hug and kiss him;[27] perhaps he had no other grandchildren.[28] As Moses grows up in the palace, Pharaoh's daughter cares for him like a son[29] and Pharaoh relates to him as a beloved grandchild.[30] Moses dresses as royalty[31] and is included in all official banquets, where he is seated in a place of honor to the left of the king.[32]

---

24. Josephus, *Antiquities of the Jews* 2:9:7.
25. It is tempting to use this approach to explain the underlying reason that Batya is at the banks of the Nile. One could suggest that she is hoping to find a baby to rescue, adopt, and raise as her own, but this notion is incongruous with the text, which clearly states that she goes to the river to bathe.
26. Exodus Rabba 1.
27. Ibid.
28. The Zohar 3:34 claims that Batya herself was a foundling, the twin sister of Moses's wife Zipporah. Perhaps Pharaoh has no biological children, either. Just as he adopted a foundling, he allows his daughter to do so.
29. *Yalkut Shimoni* on Exodus 168.
30. *Tanḥuma*, Exodus 8.
31. *Otzar HaMidrashim*, 146.
32. Ibid., 356.

Midrashic commentators conclude that Batya is a firstborn child.[33] During the tenth plague, all firstborns, both male and female, are slated to die. She is in mortal danger and Moses prays for God to have mercy on her. Indeed, her life is spared.[34] The supposition that Batya leaves Egypt with the Jewish Exodus indicates that she has no other children, nothing to leave behind.

Some commentators maintain that it is God's plan for Moses to be raised among leaders.[35] He is spared the slave mentality that is ingrained in the Israelites as a result of their extended period of humiliation and bondage. Instead, Moses interacts with influential people,[36] learning the skills necessary to shepherd a nation. This places him in a position of respect and authority in the eyes of his fellow Jews.[37] It is highly ironic that Pharaoh raises and bestows all the royal trappings on the boy about whom it was accurately foretold would eventually bring about his empire's collapse and his own personal destruction.[38] Batya's character starkly contrasts with her depraved, despotic father. She is extremely successful in instilling impeccable moral standards in her adopted son.

Moses eventually grows up and one day strolls out of the palace, where he happens upon an Egyptian slave master beating a Jewish slave. Heroically, Moses defends the abused Jew by killing his attacker and burying him in the sand. The following day, he sees a skirmish between two men, described as his brothers, and pleads with them to stop. One of the combatants objects to Moses's interference and threatens to expose him as the murderer of the Egyptian from the day before, leading Moses to hastily flee Egypt for Midian (Ex. 2:11). There he protects the daughters of Jethro from menacing shepherds.

Where does he learn to stand up for the oppressed? How does he know that the Jews are his people? Undoubtedly, these are lessons learned at the knee of his adoptive mother, Batya. Moses is born with a special soul, but it needs to be developed and nurtured. His outstand-

33. *Pesikta DeRav Kahana* 7.
34. Ibid.
35. Ibn Ezra on Exodus 2:3.
36. *Pirkei DeRabbi Eliezer* 47.
37. Ibn Ezra on Exodus 2:3.
38. Exodus Rabba 1.

ing qualities are molded under the influence of this remarkable woman who teaches Moses compassion and responsibility. In I Chronicles 4:18, this often overlooked woman reappears. We find here the textual source of the name Bitya, or Batya, meaning "daughter of God." It is possible that this is her given name, since Pharaoh thought himself to be a god. Alternatively, perhaps she converts and chooses the name for herself. Midrashic sources claim that the name originated with God Himself: "Just as Moses was not really your son, yet you raised him as one, so I will call you My daughter" (Megilla 13a).

The same verse in I Chronicles lists Batya's children's names, which correspond to Moses's different names. Despite the fact that Batya is not Moses's birth mother, the Torah attributes his birth to her because she is the one who raises him. What is fascinating about this verse is that it maintains, almost presumptively, that Batya throws her lot in with the ragtag band of migrant Jewish slave-refugees, remains connected to them, and flees her homeland with the nascent Jewish nation. She builds a new life while retaining her role as mother of Moses.

In I Chronicles, Batya is said to have married Mered (which translates literally as "rebellion"). Talmudic commentators identify Mered as the biblical figure Caleb.[39] As a member of the group of spies charged with infiltrating Canaan, he also defies societal expectations and rebels against accepted norms. Ten of the twelve scouts return with a negative report about the Jews' military prospects there, while Caleb defiantly insists that they can capture the land. Caleb and Batya are two strong personalities united in their courage to go against the grain and, despite great personal risk, they remain firm in their beliefs.

Batya is included in a list of women who are considered righteous,[40] who converted, and who even entered Gan Eden alive.[41] There is a well-known statement that it was the women of that generation who were responsible for initiating the redemption.[42] We are accustomed to associating this tremendous honor with the Jewish mothers, who continued

39. See Megilla 13a and Leviticus Rabba 1.
40. *Yalkut Shimoni.*
41. *Otzar HaMidrashim*, 162.
42. Exodus Rabba 1:16.

to bear children despite all odds. But perhaps we should apply this statement to the woman who defied her father and raised Moses to be the great leader that he became.

God's name does not appear at all in these verses (Ex. 2:1–11), but He is very much present in the actions of the people. The Torah is given to the Israelites by a man raised by an unusual barren woman – and perhaps she is the one who can take credit for the birth of the nation.

Chapter 7

Michal

In the late 1980s, a remarkable phenomenon was observed among female Cambodian refugees who had come to the United States. A large percentage of these women were visually impaired to the point of being legally blind, yet there was no physiological explanation for their handicap. It was diagnosed as psychosomatic blindness. The cure lay with psychologists rather than traditional medical practitioners. It was determined that these women had been exposed to such horrifying traumas and had witnessed such unending cruelty and brutality that their brains simply "switched off" their eyes so they could no longer witness the killing fields of Pol Pot.

Emotional trauma can have a powerful effect on a person's physical well-being and may directly influence their behavior. This is the key to understanding Michal, the daughter of King Saul and wife of King David.

Michal is the biblical character who should have lived the proverbial "happily ever after": she is a princess, the first daughter of one king and the wife of another, a woman who marries her beloved. And yet, she is one of the more tragic figures in the Bible. Michal leads a joyless, bitter, lonely life until her melancholy end.

The Beginning

The Philistines and the mammoth Goliath invade Israel. In a desperate measure,[1] King Saul offers his daughter to anyone with enough courage and skill to vanquish the fearsome giant warrior (I Sam. 17:25). Shockingly, David, a young civilian, heroically slays Goliath with his legendary slingshot, leading the Israelites to victory while simultaneously earning King Saul's resentment and loathing. King Saul grudgingly offers Merab to David as his reward, but with a twist. Saul's plan is to draft David into the royal armed forces in the hopes that he will die on the battlefield. If all goes according to plan, the king will rid himself of his enemy without getting his hands dirty (I Sam. 18:17). David rejects the offer to become the king's son-in-law, explaining that he is a commoner whose family is neither illustrious nor rich enough to marry royalty (I Sam. 18:18). Having been rebuffed by David, Merab marries Adriel the Meholathite.[2]

When King Saul realizes that his initial scheme for destroying David has been thwarted, he hatches an alternative plan. He offers David his beautiful younger daughter, Michal (Megilla 15a), who has fallen in love with the shepherd boy of questionable lineage (I Sam. 18:20). King Saul is not motivated by fatherly love or his responsibility to fulfill the pledge he has made; he gives Michal to David in order to achieve his own goal. Saul puts his plot into action by telling his friends and servants to convince David that he does not need a large dowry, that the king genuinely wants him as a son-in-law, and that all he needs to do is kill one hundred enemy Philistines (I Sam. 18:22). Clearly, Saul thinks this is an impossible task that will end in David's downfall on the battlefield. His plan backfires, however, as David, showing uncommon military acumen, successfully kills double the requested number of Philistines. Saul is left with no recourse but to give Michal to David as a wife.

1. Leviticus Rabba 37.
2. There is much discussion among the commentators regarding this union. See Sanhedrin 19b, *Metzudat David*, and others.

It seems that Michal would have been pleased to marry David, since the text states twice (I Sam. 18:20, 28) that she loves him.[3] This is the only instance that we are told of a biblical woman loving anyone. Michal marries David out of love. Saul gives Michal to David to get him killed. And David – why does he agree to the king's offer this time? Does he reciprocate Michal's love? Does he have political aspirations and hope that she will be a stepping stone to the throne? Maybe he felt there was a limit to the number of times he could politely refuse the king.[4]

Much to the disappointment of King Saul, David is not killed in his foray against the Philistines. With two hundred Philistine foreskins, David wins Michal's hand in marriage (I Sam. 18:27). At this point, it is clear that God is helping David, that Michal loves him, and that Saul views him as an enemy.

The Plot Thickens

King Saul decides that he will have to get rid of David on his own and sends messengers to his home to arrest him. Michal discovers the plan, probably from the connections that she had in the palace where she grew up,[5] and is put in a difficult position, forced to choose between her husband and her father. She makes her choice and encourages David to escape. Michal places figurines in the bed, and when the messengers arrive, she informs them that David is sick and cannot accompany them to the palace. When they bring this message to the king, he commands them to bring him anyway. If he is going to kill David, what difference does it make if he is sick or not? The messengers return to David's house to find him gone and a dummy in the bed in his place.

Saul confronts Michal, asking why she betrayed him (I Sam. 29:17). Michal responds that David threatened to kill her if she did not aid him.[6] Since she is the one who initiates David's flight, we wonder why she tells her father this lie. Perhaps she is trying to mitigate the

3. Her love for David plays an important role in the story.
4. Ralbag on II Samuel 1:27.
5. Radak on I Samuel 18:25.
6. *Midrash Tehillim* 59.

damage she has done by allowing her father's enemy to escape. She seems to want to maintain some semblance of a relationship with her father, yet Saul has no qualms about turning his daughter into a widow by murdering the man she loves.

Why does David leave Michal behind and not take her with him into exile? On a practical level, by remaining behind, she buys David extra time by sending Saul's messengers back to the palace before they return to take him from his bed.[7] In addition, as a trained warrior, David is probably much faster than Michal, who would only slow him down. However, remaining at home means that she is left to face her father's wrath alone.

Part of Michal's technique in fooling her father's messengers is placing teraphim, statues, in the bed. What is the nature of these statues? The only other time the Torah uses this term is in Genesis (31:34), in reference to the gods of Laban. Were there idols in the house of David? Nahmanides explains that not all of these teraphim were used for idol worship, and had they been gods, Michal would not have used them for mundane purposes.[8] Today, we have photographs; in those days, women kept artistic statues in their homes in honor of their loved ones.[9] Michal kept an artistic rendition of David in the house, pointing again to her love for him. Statues, though, do not have hair. To solve this problem, she used what the verse describes as *kvir ha'izim* (I Sam. 19:13), a braid of goat hair or hide with hair attached to mimic human hair. Here we see Michal's determination in saving David, and proof of her love for him.[10] We also see her intelligence in manipulating the situation to buy David more time and somehow preserve her relationship with her father. She also appears to be practical and a creative problem solver. She saves herself and David, and therefore, she ultimately saves David's most famous descendant: the Messiah.

7. Abrabanel on I Samuel 19.
8. Nahmanides on Genesis 31:19.
9. Abrabanel on I Samuel 1:13.
10. *Midrash Tehillim* 59.

Yet now she is alone, having rebelled against her father and essentially estranging herself from him, and sending her husband away to a protracted exile.

The root of the name Michal is not clear. The term appears in Prophets as a brook of water, while some suggest that it is the feminine version of the angel Michael.[11] Both of these explanations connect Michal to a life-giving source. Given her ability and power, the name Michal could also be a contraction of the phrase *Mi yakhel la*, "Who can possibly overcome her?" Based on this story, perhaps it is Michal who, in saving David's life, becomes a messenger of God and a source of life to the world.

Marriage

The text continues with the story of David. We hear of his marriages to Abigail and Ahinoam, and discover that King Saul has given Michal to Palti the son of Laish, who is from Galim (I Sam. 14:44). We are not told that anyone asks Michal if she wants a new arrangement. How can Saul take away David's wife and give her to another man? Saul rules that David and Michal's marriage is invalid. According to halakha, marriage requires a transfer of something of monetary value from the groom to the bride. Saul determines that foreskins have no monetary value, and so the marriage is nullified; Michal is therefore free to marry someone else.[12] In the same fashion, one of Saul's advisors, Doeg the Edomite, considers David's marriage to Michal invalid because David is declared a rebel against the king and therefore already considered dead. Either way, Saul no longer deems Michal and David's marriage to be legitimate. Why does Saul revisit the status of the marriage now? Perhaps he is angry that David has taken other wives.

Alternatively, some commentators suggest that Michal is not given to Paltiel as a wife, but rather as a prisoner.[13] The verse simply states that Saul "gave" her, which could perhaps be interpreted as giving

11. *Daat Mikra* on I Samuel 14:49 [Hebrew] (Mossad HaRav Kook).
12. Tosefta on Sota 11:19.
13. Abrabanel on I Samuel 19.

her as a hostage. In this view, Saul punishes Michal for her betrayal and decides to banish her, providing a jailer, Palti, to take care of her needs. Michal the princess is being held in a tower with a guard protecting her.

Reunification of the Kingdom

In time, the kingdom of Saul disintegrates and that of David rises to power. Saul is now dead and his son, Ish-bosheth, is a ruler of sorts. Abner, the head of Ish-bosheth's army, feels rejected because Ish-bosheth has refused his request to marry Saul's concubine. He secretly approaches David with an offer to bring the remaining followers of Saul to his camp. David agrees on one condition: that Abner bring Michal. David also decides to go through proper diplomatic channels and puts in an official request to Ish-bosheth, saying, "Give me my wife Michal, for whom I paid a bride-price of a hundred Philistine foreskins" (II Sam. 3:14). When David requests her return, he specifies that he married her legitimately, mentioning the foreskins to preempt anyone who tries to invalidate his original marriage.

Why is David asking for Michal now? Nine years have passed since the night Michal saved him: two years on the run and seven years in Hebron. Has there been no possibility of reuniting with her before this? From a political standpoint, reuniting with Michal is of tremendous benefit to David. There is no better way to reunite the nation than for the new king to marry into the old regime – and hopefully produce a descendant who will rule with the authority of both families. On the other hand, at this point David has other wives and Michal no longer plays the prominent role as preferred first wife. Perhaps David is suspicious of Abner and hopes that because Michal was previously a reliable source of insider information, she will now verify whether this is a legitimate offer or a trick.

No one asks Michal for her preference, and it is clear that she is being used as a political pawn to advance David's rule over the whole nation. Ish-bosheth takes her from Paltiel, who is described as following her, crying, until they reach Bahurim, at which point Abner tells him to return home.

There is much discussion among the rabbis as to the halakhic legitimacy of David "remarrying" Michal. Halakha states that if a man was married to a woman and she marries or has relations with a second man, she cannot return to the original husband. If we follow the approach that Paltiel is just her guardian, we avoid this difficult issue; perhaps he cries when she leaves because he has become fond of her over the nine years. If, however, Michal was indeed married to Paltiel, how could David take her back?

A number of suggestions are put forward. The most famous is that of the Midrash, which explains that Paltiel knows that Michal is married to David, and so he is careful to remain physically apart from her, to the extent that he places a sword outside her door as a reminder to keep his distance.[14] It is possible that Paltiel's motivation is not necessarily halakhic, but rather that he is wise enough to know not to cross David. Either way, the Midrash compares Paltiel to Joseph and Boaz, placing him on an even higher level: Joseph and Boaz are both tempted once and escape, but Paltiel lives with constant temptation for years and still does not sin.[15] In this scenario, he cries when Michal leaves because he knows that he is losing a source of reward that will be impossible to match. He cries until he reaches the place called Bahurim, meaning "youth," which hints that his relationship with Michal was a youthful, innocent friendship rather than that of lovers. Indeed, when Michal is removed from the home of Paltiel, the verse (II Sam. 3:15) reads: *Me'im ish, me'im Paltiel ben Laish,* "[Ish-bosheth sent and had her taken away] from her husband, from Paltiel son of Laish."

The term *ish,* "man," rather than *baal,* "husband," is used to describe Paltiel. When Michal is initially given to Palti, his name is spelled without the *el.* In this chapter, he is called Paltiel, adding the name of God (*El*) as a stamp of innocence and righteousness (Sanhedrin 19b). Palti comes from the root P-L-T, denoting a refugee or survivor, and he is a refugee saved from temptation and sin with God as his witness.

Radak offers three opinions as to how David can reunite with Michal, but then rejects all of them. First, one could argue that this

14. Radak on I Samuel 25:43.
15. Leviticus Rabba 23.

arrangement is indeed invalid, a sin. Second, as suggested earlier, Michal and David's original marriage may not have been valid because David did not give her anything of value to secure the marriage. Third, perhaps Palti and Michal never consummate their marriage. Rejecting these explanations, Radak's choice answer is that Saul forces David to divorce Michal on one of his visits back to the kingdom, in order to save her from becoming an *aguna*, a woman who is "chained" to her marriage. A forced bill of divorce is not valid, but as no one knows that it is forced, Michal and Palti get married based on it. Since they "sin" unknowingly, based on a misunderstanding, Michal is not forbidden to her husband.[16]

Alternatively, one could posit that if David wants her back merely as a political pawn, he may not be interested in a physical relationship. This explanation avoids the halakhic problem altogether.

Joy?

After many years of wandering, David brings the Ark of God up to Jerusalem. There is tremendous joy and happiness in finally performing this important mitzva. David, wearing a garment described as similar to a linen apron or skirt such as the priests wore, dances ecstatically in front of the entire nation. While crowds join in the celebrations in the street with singing and dancing, Michal remains indoors watching the ceremony through the window. She sees David "leaping and dancing before the Lord" and feels contempt for him in her heart.[17]

The Ark is brought to its designated place; David offers sacrifices, then blesses the whole nation and distributes gifts. Not waiting until David arrives home, Michal goes out to greet him in the street. In a scornful manner, she says: "How dignified the king of Israel was today, exposing himself before all the eyes of his servants' slave girls just as one of the rabble might expose himself" (II Sam. 6:20). David answers: "It was before the Lord, who chose me instead of your father and all his

16. Radak on I Samuel 25:43. This is similar to the situation of a woman who is raped; she may return to her husband because she is not at fault.
17. The same term expressing contempt is used in Genesis 25:34 to describe Esau mocking his birthright before selling it.

household, and appointed me as ruler over the Lord's people, Israel.... I danced before the Lord. And I would have lowered myself even further and been humiliated in my own eyes – but to the slave girls you speak of, I would still be dignified" (II Sam. 6:21–22).

Michal finds David's behavior completely inappropriate and even demeaning to him and his position. David's response is insensitive and insulting, telling her that God chose him over her family for a reason.

Regarding another public celebration, Maimonides describes the festivities that occurred in the Temple with cymbals:[18]

> [In addition] each person would play the instrument he knew. Those who could sing would sing. They would dance and clap their hands, letting loose and whistling, each individual according to his ability. Words of song and praise were recited.... It was a great mitzva to maximize this celebration. The common people and anyone who desired would not perform [in these celebrations]; only the greatest of Israel's wise men: the heads of the yeshivot, the members of the high court, the pious, the elders, and the men of stature. They were those who would dance, clap their hands, sing, and rejoice in the Temple on the days of the festival of Sukkot. However, the entire people – the men and the women – would come to see and hear.... The happiness with which a person should rejoice in the fulfillment of the mitzvot and the love of God who commanded them is a great service. Anyone who lowers himself and thinks lightly of his person in these situations is [truly] a great person, worthy of honor, who serves God out of love. Thus, David, king of Israel, declared [II Sam. 6:22]: "I would have lowered myself even further and been humiliated in my own eyes," because there is no greatness or honor other than celebrating before God, as the verse states [II Sam. 6:16]: "King David was dancing wildly and whistling before God."

David, inspired by holiness, ignores his high position and dances in wild ecstasy before God.

18. Maimonides, *Sefer Zemanim, Hilkhot Shofar VeSukka VeLulav* 8:14.

Halakha requires spiritual leaders to be role models in the realm of loving God. This love should be expressed with no self-consciousness, precisely through the negation of the self by dancing and singing emotionally before one's Creator. Michal does not understand this kind of behavior. She finds it demeaning and undignified for the king.[19] Perhaps Michal, like the blind women of Cambodia, shuts down a part of her brain that deals with emotion. Having been used as a pawn from the beginning, swapped between people she had relationships with based on the whims of others, she copes by closing down her emotional outlet. When she sees David expressing his love of God through purely emotional devotion, she cannot understand or relate to his behavior.

The next verse tells us that "Michal, Saul's daughter, never had a child – to her dying day" (II Sam. 6:23). This seamless continuation indicates that it is a direct result of the earlier verse.[20] It could be that she has no children because once she shuts down emotionally, her body also shuts down physically, at least in the sense that she cannot conceive.

Michal is never referred to as barren, yet there is no mention of children other than this verse. Abrabanel considers it a great kindness of God, given what would happen in the future: The Gibeonites ask for seven of Saul's descendants to kill. If Michal had children, they would have been murdered. The verse states that five of these victims are the sons of Adriel the Meholatite and Michal. We know that Michal had no children, certainly not with Adriel; the verse is actually speaking about Merab, Michal's sister. The commentators reconcile this discrepancy by explaining that Merab died prematurely and Michal stepped in to help raise her nephews. As a result, Scripture attributes them to her. Raising children is viewed as equal to birthing them (Sanhedrin 19b). If this is indeed so, it supports our theory of emotional shutdown as a coping mechanism.

According to the simplest reading, it is clear that Michal is barren. Is this a result of a physical problem? Do her suppressed emotions prevent her ability to conceive? Or is she childless because she does not have a physical relationship with her husband, whether because of

19. Ralbag on II Samuel 6:16.
20. Ralbag on II Samuel 6:20.

halakhic considerations or emotional issues?[21] Perhaps it is psychological? Is it a punishment?[22]

Another reading of this verse suggests that Michal has no children *until* she dies – in other words, she dies in childbirth.[23] The Gemara comments on a list of David's sons that appears in the text. We are told that David has children in Hebron: his firstborn, Amnon, born to Ahinoam, then Chileab to Abigail, followed by Absalom born to Maacah, then Adonijah born to Haggith, Shephatiah born to Abital, and finally, the sixth son on the list is Ithream, born to "Eglah, David's wife" (II Sam. 3:5). One opinion in the Gemara says that Eglah is in fact Michal, and so Ithream is Michal's son.[24]

However, if we take the view that Michal is childless, that would mean that she is unable to continue her father's lineage, dashing any hopes of unifying the kingdoms of Saul and David. That would probably influence her standing among the king's wives.

Some say that Michal is a reincarnation of a man (Eiruvin 96a). The Gemara states that she wore tefillin and no one reprimanded her (Eiruvin 96a.). Perhaps she gives up on her relationship with humanity and instead develops a relationship with God. If she is in the tower, so to speak, what does she do all day? Have her emotional capacity and female traits disappeared?

It is interesting to compare the stories of Michal and the matriarch Rachel.[25] Both of their fathers wish to harm their future husbands, tricking them by offering one sister but actually giving the second. In both situations, the husband pays double what is required of him. Both husbands are forced to run away, but in time, the fathers try to reconcile with their sons-in-law. Jacob and David both demand that their wives

---

21. Ralbag on II Samuel 6:20.
22. Ralbag on II Samuel 21:21.
23. Rashi on II Samuel 3:5 says that Michal didn't have children until the day she died – meaning that she died in childbirth.
24. Why was Michal called Eglah (literally, "calf")? Because she bleated like a calf during childbirth (*Midrash Shmuel* 22) or because David loved her like a pet (Rashi on I Chr. 3:3).
25. Rabbi Yaakov Medan, *David and Batsheva* [Hebrew] (Alon Shvut: Tvunot Publishing House, 2002), 121–126.

be returned to them, and they question why they were tricked. It is also interesting that the term "teraphim," "statues," appears only in these two stories. The most obvious similarity, however, lies in the women's barrenness. We know that Rachel feels that without a child, her life is meaningless. While we don't have a record of what Michal thinks or feels, as we suggested earlier, it seems that she too gives up on a normal life.

Not all princesses live happily ever after. With her position, Michal should have been happy, but once she becomes a pawn in the political manipulations of the people around her, she can no longer enjoy the privileges of royal life.

Chapter 8

Tamar, Daughter of David

Sonnet 129

Th' expense of spirit in a waste of shame
is lust in action; and till action, lust
is perjured, murd'rous, bloody, full of blame,
savage, extreme, rude, cruel, not to trust,
enjoyed no sooner but despisèd straight;
past reason hunted; and, no sooner had,
past reason hated as a swallowed bait,
on purpose laid to make the taker mad;
mad in pursuit, and in possession so;
had, having, and in quest to have, extreme;
a bliss in proof, and proved, a very woe;
before, a joy proposed; behind, a dream.
All this the world well knows; yet none knows well
to shun the heaven that leads men to this hell.

In this sonnet Shakespeare describes a lust that turns to hate. The temporary sensual thrill quickly dissipates with feelings of emptiness, sadness, and guilt. While it is unknown what motivated Shakespeare to author this sonnet, one can empathize with the portrait of agony and desolation that he paints.

This sonnet of longing that metamorphizes into loathing is the perfect description of the story of Tamar and Amnon: a story that begins with rape and incest in the House of David, and ends with murder (II Sam. 13:1).

The Narrative

The chapter begins with a description of Tamar, the beautiful sister of Absalom, son of King David.[1] Amnon, also the son of the king, loves her. Amnon is David's firstborn son with Ahinoam (II Sam. 3:2). Absalom is next in line[2] to inherit the throne; his mother is Maacah, daughter of the king of Geshur (II Sam. 3:3). The stage is set for the conflict between the king's descendants, with Tamar somehow caught in the middle.

Absalom is described as the most exceptionally handsome man in the kingdom (II Sam. 14:25–27). There must have been an unusually beautiful genetic composition present in the family, as it is exceedingly rare for Scripture to single out a man for his appearance. A careful reading of the verse indicates that Tamar and Absalom are brother and sister, while Amnon is a half-sibling. According to the Gemara (Sanhedrin 21a), their mother Maacah was a *yefat toar* (Deut. 21:10–14), a beautiful woman, possibly captured by David on the battlefield. According to biblical law, a soldier may have intimate relations with such a woman one time, and then he brings her home. The soldier then waits a month, at which point the woman either converts to Judaism and marries him or is sent back to her home. Tamar is never explicitly referred to as the daughter of David. This could be because Maacah is already pregnant when she comes out to entice the men on the battlefield.[3] Another explanation is that because Maacah is a convert,[4] her child retains none of her previous family relationships.[5] Abrabanel rejects this idea, stating that there

1. She is not called the daughter of David.
2. Chileab son of Abigail is actually the second in line, but he disappears from the text.
3. See *Tosafot*. According to this opinion, Tamar has no biological connection to Amnon.
4. See Rashi on II Samuel 13:13 and Maimonides, *Sefer Shofetim, Hilkhot Melakhim UMilḥemoteihem* 8:8.
5. Ralbag on II Samuel 13:19.

is no reason to accuse David of capturing Maacah and raping her on the battlefield when that is not reported in the text.

Taking the view that Maacah married David while already pregnant with Tamar, Amnon would in fact have been an eligible and legitimate marital partner. To fend off Amnon's advances, Tamar pleads for a legal marriage to be arranged (II Sam. 13:13). Perhaps Amnon does not accede to her request because he suspects that King David will not accept it. After all, if the marriage between them were to take place, it would be like a public declaration that David is not Tamar's father.[6] Alternatively, marriage between members of the royal family may have been considered inappropriate by the outside world. More likely, Amnon is not interested in official protocol because he does not desire her for love. His interest in her is based on primal lust and the fact that she is a virgin, as indicated by the following verse.

This is not an innocent infatuation; it resembles an obsession. The Mishna cites this relationship as the paradigm of impure, conditional love.[7] It is likely that Amnon has never even interacted directly with Tamar, as the king's virgin daughters live in separate quarters in the palace.[8] It would be erroneous to view him as being in love in the classic sense, as he essentially had no way of knowing her in any meaningful way. The king's daughters were exceedingly modest and did not leave their royal chambers, adding to Amnon's difficulty in reaching her.[9]

The narrative also alludes to Amnon's incompetence; he is faced with a challenge and does not know how to address it. This reflects poorly on his prospects as a future leader. Not only is he impotent in developing a viable course of action, but instead of behaving with dispassionate objectivity, he becomes emotionally overwrought, which causes him to be physically ill. This does not bode well. How might he react when faced with a difficult and complex issue of national consequence?

6. Abrabanel on II Samuel 13:2.
7. Mishna Avot 5:15.
8. *Metzudat David* on II Samuel 13:2.
9. Radak on II Samuel 13:2.

Advice

The reader is introduced to Jehonadab, a nephew[10] and friend of the king who is also a cousin of Amnon. He is described as an exceptionally astute individual, one of the few to receive this appellation in the biblical narrative. He perceptively notices that something is amiss with Amnon and asks for an explanation, at which point Amnon professes his feelings for Tamar. Jehonadab provides him with clever advice. Amnon is to pretend to be bedridden. When the king visits him, Amnon should request that the king arrange for Tamar to help him recuperate by preparing fresh food before him to stimulate his appetite.

While Jehonadab's scheme places Amnon and Tamar in the same room, the text does not divulge the extent of Jehonadab's knowledge of the situation. Is he an accomplice to the brutal rape by suggesting a way to trick Tamar into arriving at the crime scene? It strains credulity to think that he would have entertained the outrageous possibility that Amnon intended to sexually assault his own sister. Perhaps he surmised that just being able to interact with her would have been enough for Amnon to quell his lust, especially when he realizes that she is not the stunningly beautiful woman he thought her to be.[11] Jehonadab's brilliance might be that he is careful not to implicate himself. He never suggests anything inappropriate, but does he have some sort of ulterior motive?[12] Perhaps he is turning it over to David, assuming that once David hears the request, he will see it as strange and make his own investigation.

Indeed, David does come to visit his apparently ill firstborn son and immediately, without questioning him, agrees to his bizarre request. The text recounts with a wry list of verbs how Tamar is summoned to Amnon's chambers and how she undertakes her task with a neutral, businesslike approach. She appears to be lost in a whirlwind of activity as she laconically gets the job done. Adding to the strange and awkward

---

10. II Samuel 13:3 describes him as the son of King David's brother Shimi.
11. *Kli Yakar* on II Samuel 13:3.
12. How is it that Jehonadab is at David's side when he hears about the murder of the king's sons and he knows to say, "Don't worry, it's only Absalom killing Amnon as an act of revenge"? Was he in on it all along with Absalom?

scene is the fact that she is going to a house full of servants and likely even arrived with her own entourage of servants, yet she is the only one preparing the fresh food that Amnon requests.

The Rape

Amnon refuses to eat and dismisses the staff, leaving him alone with Tamar. The unsuspecting Tamar should have left with her attendants, but in a display of unfortunate naiveté (much like her father King David), she remains alone with the predator. Amnon orders her to bring the food she prepared into his inner chamber. Then a healthy Amnon seizes her and suggests a consensual relationship. One can speculate that he hopes he will be able to force David to grudgingly approve of the marriage retroactively.

Despite being in an exceedingly difficult position, Tamar presents several logical arguments to repel Amnon's unwanted advances. Tamar, the descendant of a convert, tells Amnon that his reprehensible conduct is inappropriate in Israel[13] and that it will result in him being branded as a miscreant who is unfit to rule. She further argues that not only will he damage his own honor, he will also disgrace her. She suggests that they follow proper protocol and go to the king to receive his blessing. Tamar is very clear about the fact that she strongly opposes his advances, and that it would be ruinous for everybody involved.

It is unknown whether the king would have permitted the union; perhaps Tamar's suggestion proves that they were not blood relatives. Alternatively, maybe it is simply a desperate ploy to resist Amnon's egregious assault.[14]

Amnon rejects her suggestion and brutally rapes her.

The Aftermath

Immediately after Amnon commits his heinous crime, he becomes saturated with an intense loathing that far eclipses his initial longing for

13. *Daat Mikra* on II Samuel 13:13 [Hebrew] (Mossad HaRav Kook).
14. Abrabanel on II Samuel 13:13.

Tamar. He cannot bear to lay eyes on her for another minute and calls on his servant to toss this "thing" out and lock the door. A despondent Tamar desperately pleads with him to keep her, explaining that casting her away is a crime even worse than the rape, since a woman who has been violated has nowhere to turn. Amnon, having earlier proven to be an incompetent, helpless character, now vividly shows that he has no conscience, compassion, self-control, or sense of responsibility – certainly an exceedingly poor candidate to inherit the throne.

Ammon's longing is replaced with hate because his desire for Tamar was based purely on lust. Once he has used her to satisfy his hunger, she is no longer of any value to him. What had appealed to him was the idea that she represented; she was nothing more than a conduit for his own physical pleasure, a form of self-love. As Rabbi Joseph B. Soloveitchik explains in *On Repentance*:

> A moment before he sinned Amnon surely still thought that Tamar represented beauty of which there was none higher, none more splendorous or glorious. This filled him with such powerful love that because of it he sinned and did "this base deed... as one of the base men." This was the case before the sin, but immediately afterward: "And Amnon hated her with a great hatred, for the hatred with which he hated her was greater than the love with which he had loved her" (II Sam. 13:15).[15]

He hates her now with such a vengeance not because he suffers pangs of conscience, but because in his eyes, she suddenly becomes ugly and repulsive. His sin is an abomination to him. Sin has a masochistic effect: Amnon hates himself and transfers his hatred to Tamar, humiliated through no fault of her own. The sense of bereavement that comes from sin is expressed in feelings of defilement, loathing, and self-hatred. Amnon has no time for reason, and neither the mind nor the intellect is responsible for the transformation that occurred in his soul, turning love into hate, desire into revulsion. These emotions come as an instinctive

15. Rabbi Soloveitchik, *On Repentance*, ed. Pinchas Peli (Oroth Publishing House: 1980), 216–218.

reaction to the sin. Tamar could not have understood that this was the natural reaction of the sinner to the sin itself, as well as to the object of his sin. Amnon now identifies Tamar with his sin, the symbol of his failure. His animus toward her reflects the depth of his self-hatred over his inability to resist temptation. As Shakespeare alludes to in Sonnet 129, lust once acted upon "leads men to this hell."

The Gemara claims that Amnon reviles Tamar because she castrated him during the melee.[16] Ralbag suggests that his negative feelings toward her are based on the acerbic invectives that she must have heaped upon him.[17] The predator's physical and emotional wounds mirror the pain inflicted on his prey. These sources provide a small measure of power to the victim, an indication of how she violently resists.

This might clarify a seemingly incomprehensible halakha. A man who forcibly rapes a single woman is obligated to pay a fine and marry her (Deut. 22:28–29). It is for her benefit that he must marry her, as in ancient times, a woman without a male protector was left destitute. The rapist is forced to live with and support the object of his sin daily for the rest of his life. He is held accountable for his actions and must live with his own guilt, which may be even more trying than living with her.

As a result of this story, a halakha is enacted by David and his court prohibiting a man and woman from being secluded together in a private domain.[18] Originally, the halakha only applied to men and married women, where the risk of a liaison carries with it the severe penalties of adulterers. Following the incident with Tamar and Amnon, the prohibition was extended to include all women.

Conclusion

Following the abominable act, Amnon cannot even bring himself to utter Tamar's name. He abruptly banishes her from his room and locks the door behind her to prevent the possibility of return. He does not even

16. Sanhedrin 21a.
17. Ralbag on II Samuel 13:15.
18. Maimonides, *Sefer Kedusha, Hilkhot Issurei Bia* 22:3.

wait for the cover of darkness, which would have helped her furtively slink away to avoid embarrassment.

Tamar immediately takes on the practices of a mourner: she places ashes on her head, tears her royal garments (a *ketonet passim,* a beautiful tunic made of stripes), and cries as she walks with her hand on her head. Not willing to remain silent, she must have appeared as a madwoman, perhaps calling for revenge and justice. Absalom hears of her strange behavior and is immediately able to surmise what has happened. He orders her to remain silent, telling her that "he is your brother" after all and that she shouldn't "take it to heart" (II Sam. 13:20). Absalom is obviously planning something and does not want Tamar to call attention to his vengeful scheme. Absalom welcomes her into his home and eventually names his daughter after her (II Sam. 14:27). This is Absalom's way of giving Tamar some sort of respect and continuation while she lives in his home as a barren spinster with no hope for a future.

Revenge

Two years after the incident, Absalom defends his sister's honor by murdering Amnon at a sheep-shearing party. He then flees to his grandfather in Geshur (II Sam. 13:23–30). No one knows what Absalom's thoughts are when he executes Amnon. While it is possible that it was an act of justice for Tamar, he circumvents the formal legal process and metes out an erroneous sentence – death is not the punishment for rape. Alternatively, perhaps Absalom's goal is to eliminate any obstacles to his own claim to the throne, and he uses Tamar's rape as a pretext for killing Amnon.

King David, who is aware of the entire episode, is upset (after all, he was a major prop in the success of Amnon's evil scheme) and troubled, yet remains silent. David is guilty, inasmuch as it was his lapse in judgment that leads to Tamar being placed in such a dangerous situation. The king also realizes that had he reprimanded his rapist son, Amnon could justifiably have responded that David also succumbed to temptation. Didn't David take Bathsheba, a woman also ostensibly off-limits to him? David betrayed his officer Uriah and arranged to have him killed. Now Amnon is betrayed by his family and murdered. David may interpret the entire sequence of events as part of his punishment for his tryst with Bathsheba, and therefore grudgingly and painfully accepts the ramifications of his behavior.[19]

Our story is analogous to two other biblical stories:[20] The first is the account of Joseph, which contains the only other reference to a *ketonet passim*. Both stories feature brothers who are mired in a power struggle, both Tamar and Joseph are good-looking, both are victims of unwanted advances, and in both scenarios, the *ketonet passim* represents a loss of innocence. Tamar and Joseph are essentially imprisoned following their attacks. There are also textual parallels between the two accounts. The obvious major difference is that in one story, the victim is a male, and in the other, the victim is a female. It is no coincidence that in writing the book of Samuel, Gad the prophet alludes to the Joseph story, using Joseph as a foil to Amnon. Joseph holds himself to a higher standard and steadfastly refuses to surrender to his evil inclination, an example that Amnon would have done well to follow.

The other case of rape in the Bible is that of Jacob's daughter Dina, who is attacked by Shechem son of Hamor the Hivite, and here too we find textual similarities between the two narratives. In both cases, the perpetrator claims to love the victim. Both women have fathers who are silent and brothers who avenge their honor while they are told to keep quiet. However, we see that Amnon is even more morally reprehensible than the gentile Shechem. At the very least, Shechem is willing to marry Dina, whereas Amnon throws Tamar out.

Tamar spends the rest of her days as a shattered, ruined woman protected by her generous brother Absalom. There is no mention of her marrying and having children. It is surprising that someone from the royal family, lauded by Scripture as beautiful, is unable to find a mate, even after the incident with Amnon. Perhaps Tamar suffered from psychological trauma as a result of the rape, precluding her from entering into a long-term relationship with another man.

---

19. Radak on II Samuel 13:15.
20. Yigal Ariel, *Oz Melekh* [Hebrew] (Diram Books, 1995), 208–209.

Anna's Story: A Jewish Legacy

By Anna Olswanger

I was fifty-five years old when I married in 2009. I knew I was too old to give birth or adopt. I often cried because I didn't have children.

A few months into my marriage, I sat in a movie theater and watched as Julia Child (in *Julie & Julia*) read a letter she had received from her sister as her husband stood nearby. When she came to the part of the letter where her sister wrote that she was pregnant, Julia began to cry painfully. Her husband moved over to her, and through her crying, Julia said, "I'm so happy." Her husband answered, "I know."

Of course, both he and the viewers knew that she was not crying out of happiness for her sister, but because of her own grief over not having children.

Later at home that evening, I formed the idea of a worldwide organization for Jewish women and men who were past normal child-bearing ages and who believed they would never have children, whether biologically or by adoption. I envisioned the organization as a way to bring us together, both online and in the real world, to explore the meaning and experience of being a childless Jewish adult. And I wanted participants to help each other discover ways to create an inheritance for future generations, the way I saw Julia Child had done. She served her country during World War II in an international spy ring managed by the Office of Strategic Services, and later brought joy to millions through her cookbooks and television shows.

On the website of my new organization, I provided a short list of childless Jewish women and men who, in my opinion, left a meaningful inheritance to the Jewish people. The women included: Deborah the prophetess (eighth century BCE), referred to in the book of Judges as the "mother of Israel" without any mention of her children or family life; Lina Frank Hecht (1848–1921), a Jewish philanthropist and social reformer in Boston; Henrietta Szold (1860–1945), an American Zionist leader and founder of Hadassah Women's Organization; Sarah Schenirer (1883–1935), founder of the Bais Yaakov movement, the first Orthodox school system for girls; Clara Haskil (1895–1960), a musician living in Bucharest who was one of the most prestigious pianists of her time; and Nechama Leibowitz (1905–1997), a scholar of Jewish studies and Bible thought who changed the face of Jewish education.

I felt inspired by these women who had lived deeply meaningful lives and hoped that others would also feel inspired and explore the meaning of their own lives, despite being childless. I waited for people to visit the site and leave comments in the forum. The following is an excerpt from one post:

> Do we sometimes avoid phone calls from insensitive "friends" who just keep talking about their children, grandchildren, cousins' children, etc. in ad nauseam detail? I feel like such a *tzaddeket* just listening to all the news about people I know and some whom I never will. And what about the people who ask me how my Pesaḥ was? Of course, I say it was wonderful and meaningful. This is what people want to hear. I would never tell anyone how lonely and empty it is, or talk about the burden of Shabbat and Yom Tov.... We heard a story the other day from a non-Jewish parent who said his twenty-four-year-old son is getting married in June to his girlfriend. They have a fifteen-month-old child

> together. The father of the groom said he is happy that his son is finally getting married. Both his son and his fiancée have four-year college degrees and good jobs. I thought to myself: In Torah Judaism, who would ever think of having children before marriage? Now that I am older and childless, I see that perhaps I would have been better off having a child when I could have, even if I was single at the time, instead of "waiting" until marriage and ending up with nothing! We can only go forward and enjoy today. I am just feeling angry today.

And another post:

> Am wondering if anyone can offer me some emotional support. I thought that I would have an easier time dealing with Shabbat, Yom Tov, and the entire Orthodox lifestyle as I aged. Instead, it is increasingly difficult to live as an Orthodox Jewish older married woman in a community that is bursting with new babies born every month, new engagements, weddings, etc. I fit in nowhere, as a result of being childless. The women my age go to their married children for Pesaḥ, or their children come to them. It is truly a celebration of family life and continuity. Yes, I know with all the preparations of planning menus, shopping, cooking, and cleaning for Pesaḥ, whether young or older, all women work hard preparing and making Pesaḥ. I do too, but with great difficulty and minimal cleaning help. We went out for the *Sedarim*, which took tremendous pressure off me. I am now dealing with chronic and debilitating health issues. I use a walker or a rollator as a result of falling several times.... I feel useless as a homemaker, and am no longer able to host guests for any Shabbat and Yom Tov meals. I put a lot of energy into being positive and upbeat when I am around other people. Only my husband knows of my sadness. I see

> older people many times have an adult child or another relative help them during times of chronic and acute illness. How are other older, childless orphans dealing with illness when there is no family support in any way? I have no close friends because I am different, not having children and grandchildren.... And if you do not reciprocate with Shabbat and Yom Tov meal invitations, people eventually stop inviting you, even though we bring a very nice hostess gift.... I live with such loneliness, which itself only exacerbates the physical challenges I have.

Post after post was filled with sadness. That was not what I had envisioned in starting the site. I had wanted it to provide hope, to encourage women to create a legacy without children. No one has posted on the site since 2017, and only occasionally do I visit it now. The idea of a community of childless Jews coming together to explore what legacy they could leave to the Jewish people never got off the ground. I didn't find my community, and in the intervening years, I have continued to experience moments of overwhelming sadness at what I lost by not having children, always wondering, for example, if I would have grown into a kinder and more patient person had I been a mother.

I also continue to feel like an outsider in my local Jewish community, especially on holidays when children are so much a part of the celebrations, and even during Kiddush after davening, when the young parents are distracted by their children, and the parents my age are focused on talking to their grandchildren or can only talk about their grandchildren.

As I move into the last part of my life, I want to reckon with my feelings. I love being Jewish and don't want to squander one more minute feeling frustrated or sad about any aspect of it. I know instinctively that creativity is the essence of life, which is why having children is so important, but is having children the only way of expressing human creativity? What if there is creativity in everything we do, whether in giving birth, starting a business, cooking a new recipe, solving a math problem, or writing computer code? I regret that I didn't get married at an earlier age and have children, but I can express my creativity – most importantly, as a Jew – despite being childless.

I see this world as a symphony. We each have our own instrument to play and I have mine. I may not feel that I am part of my local Jewish community, but I am part of the wider Jewish community, the community where I am a writer of books, many of them for children, and all of them Jewish-themed. This is a community where what I do feels important.

As I was polishing these words, October 7 happened. It soon became clear that the brutal attack on Israel was an attack on all Jews. Now, when I stand for Israel, I am standing for the Jews in Israel and the ones in my local community, the Jews who are religious and the ones who are liberal, the Jews who have children and the ones who are childless. The barriers are down.

I hope that after the war, the barriers will stay down.

Anna Olswanger lives in the metro New York area, where she is a literary agent and author. Her most recent book is the graphic novel *A Visit to Moscow*, a 2023 Eisner Award nominee about a 1965 trip to the Soviet Union by Rabbi Rafael Grossman.

Part Three

Women Who Fight for or Lose Their Children

ראתה כי מת בנה

(II Kings 11:1)

Chapter 9

The Judgment of Solomon

In an episode of the American sitcom *Seinfeld*, two of the main characters, Elaine and Kramer, are fighting over ownership of a bicycle. Unable to reach a decision, another character, Newman, acts as judge and threatens to cut the bicycle in half. Kramer doesn't want the bike to be damaged and gives up his claim, after which Newman announces that Kramer is obviously the rightful owner – a humorous application of the judgment of Solomon.

Throughout Jewish history, mothers have been forced to make difficult decisions in order to save their children. In 1938, the British government decided to allow unaccompanied Jewish minors to find safety in England. Nearly ten thousand children were saved through the Kindertransport. The courage these parents somehow found in order to send their children away to an unknown land, entrusting them to strangers so that they could live, is beyond comprehension.

In Solomon's first act as king, he is asked to adjudicate an apparently difficult case. The purpose of the story is to demonstrate the wisdom and justice promised to him by God in a dream (I Kings 3:11). He maintains truth even for the downtrodden, who have no one to defend them and have no concrete proof for their story.

Two unnamed women come to the king. They explain that they live together and that no one else was in the house with them. Both women gave birth within days of each other. The first woman claims that the other woman's baby died during the night, and she switched him with her live baby. The second woman claims that the reverse is true. This is a case that has no witnesses or evidence; it consists of two directly opposing claims.

After the first woman tells her tale and the second woman insists that it is her child who is alive, Solomon repeats both positions.[1] According to Malbim, if one pays close attention to their words, it is possible to see who the real mother is: She is the one who says, "My son lives and hers is dead." She talks about the live child first. The accuser says, "Hers is dead and mine is alive," proving that the death is on her mind.[2] Abrabanel wonders why a woman might steal a baby, initiate a court case, and be willing to have a child killed. Is she perhaps responsible for the baby's death?[3] Maybe it wasn't the accident she claims it to be. The woman telling the story claims that her baby was stolen in the night, but she also admits to sleeping, so at best her story is conjecture.

Solomon offers his judgment. He calls for a sword and declares a compromise: the child will be cut in two, and each woman will receive half.

If we look at this story from the women's perspective, we can clearly see the maternal instinct in both women. The true mother shows compassion and devotion to the infant, while the accuser is willing to lie and go to court for the chance of having a child to raise. According to the text, these women are prostitutes (I Kings 3:16). This is relevant because it explains why they live alone and have no male protector in a patriarchal society, and why they come to court by themselves. It may also highlight the strength of the maternal instinct that is present even in what we would consider the fringe of society. Motherhood is not connected to wealth or status.

Yet when Solomon offers to kill the child, one mother accepts. Why? One theory is that these two women are actually a mother-in-law

---

1. This is a halakhic requirement of a judge. See *Shulḥan Arukh, Ḥoshen Mishpat* 17:7.
2. Malbim on I Kings 3:22.
3. Abrabanel on I Kings 3:24.

and daughter-in-law, whose husbands died while they were pregnant.[4] In this scenario, it is the daughter-in-law's child who has died; she is the accuser. If she has no living child and her mother-in-law has a living son, she would be subject to *yibum* – levirate marriage, in which a man is called upon to marry his deceased brother's wife – or *ḥalitza,* the ceremony that the brother and widow can perform in order to release the duty of marriage. However, she will have to wait until the child is at least thirteen. The living baby, who is her dead husband's brother, locks her in a situation that effectively keeps her chained for many years. When Solomon offers to kill the child, it frees her from the bonds of *yibum*, and also from potentially having to raise a child that is not hers.

Does Solomon's judgment really show greatness on his part? Does he deduce who the real mother is, or does he simply expose the one with more compassion? Is it fair to put the true mother in a position of such fear?[5] Perhaps, in a state of panic, she would have frozen, unable to react. Or perhaps the woman realizes that Solomon would never kill a child, and she calls his bluff.

Putting aside the technicalities of the story, what is of significance to us is that the real mother is the woman who is willing to go to the extreme of giving up her child if it means that he will have a chance of survival. Indeed, through the centuries, motherhood has forced women to make terrible choices.

---

4. *Yalkut Shimoni* 2:175.
5. *Midrash Tehillim* 72 says it was wrong of Solomon to suggest that the child be killed.

Chapter 10

The Wife of Obadiah

In the great epic of ancient Mesopotamia, Gilgamesh, the hero mourning his friend, uses the metaphor

> And like a lioness deprived of her cubs
> he keeps pacing to and fro[1]

It seems that the lioness has been the model of the protective mother for centuries. Apparently, a lioness will often stand up and fight even the larger, stronger male lions in order to protect her offspring. A woman who defends her children against all threats is therefore often likened to a lioness.

The lioness in II Kings 4 does not have a name. We know her only as one of the wives of a prophet. She turns to Elisha crying that her husband, one of Elisha's disciples, has died, leaving her with no money to pay the creditor who wants to take her children as slaves (II Kings 4:1). This widow calls out to Elisha knowing that he looks out for his students.

1. *Epic of Gilgamesh*, Tablet 8.

This is the personal story of an individual family whom Elisha helps; this is neither a story of a national issue nor one of grave importance.

The Story

At first glance, it seems that this woman simply has a financial problem. She does not have the funds to repay a debt, for which her children may be taken in lieu of payment. However, there is an emphasis in the text about her husband and his "fear of God" that is familiar to Elisha and indicates that there may be more to the story.

The Personalities

This unnamed woman is identified as the wife of Obadiah, the prophet in charge of King Ahab's household.[2] During Ahab's reign, there is a terrible famine. Jezebel, Ahab's wife, attempts to kill all the true prophets of God. In order to save these men, Obadiah hides them in caves and provides them with their basic needs (I Kings 18:1–4). Food is expensive because of its scarcity, so Obadiah has to borrow money to sustain the large number of hidden prophets.[3] The lender, according to the Sages, is Ahab's son Jehoram, an evil character who subsequently inherits the throne.

Obadiah is described as exceedingly God-fearing. There are only four biblical characters who receive this accolade: Abraham (Gen. 22:12); Joseph (Gen. 42:18); Job (1:1); and Obadiah.

In II Kings, Elisha asks his widow, "What should I do for you?" In the Bible, this is always an expression of remuneration, indicating that Elisha knows that she is indeed owed something.[4]

One might think that if this woman's children became the servants of the king, it would a step up in society, a way to get ahead in the world. But she knows the family of Ahab, and she is petrified that if her

2. Exodus Rabba 31:4.
3. *Targum Yonatan* on II Kings 4:1 says that Obadiah is careful not to take anything that belongs to Ahab.
4. Rabbi Elchanan Samet, *Pirkei Elisha* [Hebrew] (Yedioth Books, 2009), 165.

sons come into the king's sphere of influence, they will be educated in his evil ways. She emphasizes that her husband was God-fearing to stress what a travesty it would be for his sons to be raised by those who are not. The Midrash takes this further and describes Jehoram ben Ahab bemoaning his lack of success compared to his father.[5] He is told that his father's achievements were due to Obadiah, so he requests Obadiah's sons. When Obadiah's widow refuses the king, he devises another plan to accomplish his goal, to take the children by force. What this midrash explains is a more complex desire of the creditor, who is now the king. The widow is defiant and refuses to allow her sons to be drawn into the world of Ahab, who she views as the antithesis of God-fearing.

The verse in *Eshet Ḥayil* that is associated with this character is: "She watches over the conduct of her household, and she does not eat the bread of indolence" (Prov. 31:27).[6] Indeed, the woman seems to have incredible strength and chutzpa in denying the king and saving her sons from Jehoram. This story unfolds after a difficult act of desperation by the king of Moab who, according to one interpretation, sacrifices his son and heir apparent as an offering to God. This act causes God to "have a great wrath against Israel" (II Kings 3:26–27). This gentile king sacrifices to God while the Jews worship idols. Just as the king of Moab sacrifices something of significance, so this widow is sacrificing luxury and economic security for her sons because of her beliefs. In doing so, she counterbalances the king of Moab's action and removes God's wrath from the nation. R. Mani goes as far as to state that she saves the nation from destruction – hence the text calls her "a woman," meaning a very unique and special woman.[7]

It is impossible to imagine Obadiah providing food for one hundred men without his wife not only knowing about it but agreeing to it and helping with the endeavor. She refers to her dead husband as *ishi*, "my husband" (II Kings 4:1), rather than *baali*, "my master," indicating that their relationship was that of partners.[8] When Obadiah is on his

5. Yaakov Ariel, *Ḥumash HaMegidim* [Hebrew] (Jerusalem: Machon Daat Torah).
6. *Yalkut HaMekiri* on Proverbs 31:27.
7. *Tanḥuma, Ki Tisa* 5:7.
8. Rashi on Hosea 2:18.

deathbed, his wife asks him how she will survive, and he encourages her to put her trust and belief in God.[9] Indeed, God does provide. Elisha instructs her to fill all the jugs in the house, and they are miraculously filled with oil. This indicates that Obadiah provided the men in the cave not only with food, but also with oil so that they would have light.[10] At that time, lamplight might have been considered a luxury; Obadiah and his wife determined that it would make life in the cave more tolerable.

A troubling aspect of this story is that Obadiah was clearly a good and righteous man, yet his children are left to suffer, despite the fundamental principle that states: "I was once young, now I am old, yet I have never seen the righteous forsaken, with their children begging bread" (Ps. 37:25). According to the Midrash, the woman turns to God demanding that He take care of her sons.[11] She also goes to the cemetery, calling to Obadiah to rise up and help them. He goes to Abraham, Isaac, and Jacob, all of whom suggest that she turn to Elisha.[12] These midrashim seem to indicate that her case has virtue. All the powers in the world are on her side, acknowledging her righteousness. There are a number of ways for Elisha to help this woman. She is not necessarily demanding a miracle, but this may explain why the prophet chooses to perform a miracle rather than work through other methods of solving the problem.

Neighbors

This story provides us with an alarming picture of the socioeconomic dynamic in ancient Israel. Numerous times throughout the Torah, the Jews are commanded to be especially compassionate to the widow and the orphan.[13] The lender, called a *nosheh*, lends money here with interest, against biblical command (Ex. 22:24). It is also forbidden to keep collateral overnight, so how could taking children into slavery ever be allowed?

9. Radak on II Kings 4:1.
10. Radak and Malbim on II Kings 4:1.
11. *Otzar HaMidrashim*, 144.
12. Radak on II Kings 4:1.
13. See, for example, Exodus 22:21.

One also wonders where this family's neighbors are. There must be terrible hunger in the widow's home, for she has nothing. They are willing to lend her empty vessels, but why have they not helped with food? Perhaps this woman is very proud and has not allowed the neighbors to know of her plight, and the prophet sends her to knock on their doors so they will realize what is going on.

Oil

The prophet asks the woman what is in the house, and all she has left is a small jug of oil – not even cooking oil, but oil used for cosmetics. Elisha links the miracle with that which is in the woman's house. He is teaching her that she already possesses the source of the miracle,[14] and that it is the quality, not the quantity, that matters. Elisha is confirming her strength and righteousness. She had viewed that small amount as insignificant, but Elisha reassures her that in fact it is all she needs.

Hasidic masters interpret this tale as a metaphor for the soul: The widow is the pure godly soul in each person. This soul calls out to the prophet for help as it seeks the revelation of godliness in the world. The cry of "Your servant has died" represents the internal flame of love for God that has died out. The lender is the material, animalistic side of humanity that is trying to take away the children's fear and love of God and turn them into slaves of the material. The prophet represents the spirit of godliness, asking, "What is left in your house [i.e., soul]?" The soul replies that almost nothing is left of its spirituality, just one tiny spark of God. The prophet explains that the only way to reignite that spark is by bringing empty vessels – get rid of all the negative ideas that fill the body and soul, and become a humble, empty vessel for holiness.[15]

The Miracle

Although Elisha performs a miracle to help the woman, he needs to limit it. It must start from something that already exists, the amount itself is

14. Rabbi Samet, *Pirkei Elisha*, 173.
15. Menachem Mendel Schneerson, *Likkutei Siḥot* 5:332.

limited (only what fills the vessels), and it is performed in private behind closed doors. It is also limited in terms of location and time. Even a man as great as Elisha must partner with God, and God will only send the miracle once man has taken some initiative. Oil is a human creation extracted from nature. Blessings are given from the handiwork of man, not in a vacuum.[16]

Collecting Pots

Rabbi Yigal Ariel suggests that this story indicates a tremendous failing in society.[17] While Elisha is primarily interested in helping the widow, he also wants to heal the breakdown of community. By allowing the neighbors to share their vessels, they become less self-centered and more aware of those around them. Rabbi Samet, in a close textual reading, points out that the verse never tells us that the woman actually borrows any vessels.[18] Why would she ignore the directive of the prophet? Perhaps this indicates the difficulty she had with her neighbors. She may have been scared, embarrassed, or too proud to request anything from them.

Closing the Door

An important element of the miracle depends on the woman closing the door with her sons inside. Abrabanel proposes that this is done to prevent the evil eye,[19] while Malbim suggests that it is to keep out unworthy spectators.[20] As the Gemara states, blessing is found only in that which is kept private (Bava Metzia 42a).

The events of this story take place as a result of the woman's determination not to allow her sons to be raised in the house of Ahab. Elisha teaches us some important principles for educating our children: Ideas (symbolized by the vessels) can enter the home from the outside world,

16. Tosefta on Berakhot 6:13.
17. Rabbi Yigal Ariel, *Mikdash Melekh* [Hebrew] (Hispin: Midrash HaGolan, 1994), 245.
18. Rabbi Samet, *Pirkei Elisha*, 176.
19. Abrabanel ad loc.
20. Malbim on II Kings 4:4.

where dangerous influences may lurk. At a certain point you have to close the door and fill those vessels with that which comes from inside your home. In the story, the woman's sons bring her the vessels to fill and she pours from within, filling the void.

Conclusion

When the last vessel is full, the miracle ends, and the woman is now disappointed that she did not fulfill the command of the prophet. God's blessings are boundless, but we limit our ability to receive. She turns to the prophet. Does she do so because now she wants to go borrow the vessels from her neighbors? According to Radak, she turns to the prophet to question whether she needs to tithe the oil (II Kings 4:7). Ralbag says she is questioning whether she is allowed to sell this obviously holy oil for her own needs.[21] These opinions demonstrate the exceptional nature of this woman, as she recognizes the magnitude of the miracle and wants to treat it with the proper respect.

This righteous woman fights for her children, knows what she wants, and demands from the prophet the protection and sustenance that her children need.

21. Ralbag on II Kings 4:7.

Chapter 11

Rizpah

The play *Antigone,* written by Sophocles in 441 BCE, describes a king who refuses to allow the burial of a rebellious subject, Polyneices, leaving his body to be ravaged by animals, vultures, and the elements. The king's sister protests that refusing to bury Polyneices is immoral and that there are moral norms that transcend man-made dictates. She administers last rites to the body and buries him. Opposing the king's laws and acting on her moral convictions ultimately leads to her death. Some five hundred years before Sophocles, we find a similar conflict involving King David and the sons of Saul (recorded in II Sam. 21), with a very different resolution.

The Narrative

The scene is set with a famine that has plagued the land for three years (II Sam. 21:1). The Gemara teaches us that David, trying to understand why the people have been punished with this famine, investigates his subjects to determine whether they are guilty of idol worship, promiscuity, or lax interpersonal relationships, but finds them to be innocent (Yevamot 78b). Understanding that this must be a spiritual phenomenon, he seeks an explanation from God, either through prayer or the *Urim VeTummim*. David asks three questions: What was the crime, whose fault was it, and who was harmed? He receives a three-part answer: "[It is] on account of Saul and his house of bloodshed for having killed the Gibeonites" (II Sam. 21:1). God responds that the guilty party is David's predecessor, King Saul, and his crime, while unclear, is in some way connected to harming the Gibeonites.

The Gibeonites

The Gibeonites are the inhabitants of the Canaanite city of Gibeon when Joshua leads the Jews into the Land of Israel (Josh. 9). Instead of joining the rest of the Canaanites in the war against the nation of Israel, they deceive the Israelites into reaching an accord with them. They disguise themselves as people who have come from a distant kingdom and convince Joshua that they are not local citizens (whom Joshua was enjoined to destroy, convert, or expel) but sojourners from a foreign land and therefore exempt from the fate reserved for the indigenous Canaanite population. The Israelites elect to honor the treaty even after discovering that they have been duped by the tattered clothing, stale bread, and worn-out shoes, props used by the Gibeonites to make it appear that they have come from far away. Joshua maintains that despite the false pretenses, a treaty ratified in the name of God must be preserved. The Gibeonites are allowed to live among the Israelites, but they are limited to the trades of woodcutter and water carrier.

While there is no explicit biblical reference to Saul having harmed this minority group, a number of different suggestions are offered by the commentators. One proposal is that when Saul thoroughly destroys Nob, the city of priests (I Sam. 22:18–21), the Gibeonite inhabitants of the city are also killed (Y. Kiddushin 4:1). Others maintain that Saul demolishes their livelihood by annihilating the priests of Nob, with whom the Gibeonites hold important commercial dealings. The Gemara equates this with murder.[1] With both these approaches, the presumption is that the harm inflicted upon the Gibeonites is unintentional.

The difficulty with these interpretations is that a simple reading of the text leaves the reader with the impression that Saul's actions are

1. See Yevamot 78b and Bava Kamma 119a.

far less benign. The prophet recounts that God tells King David that the famine is in response to King Saul's "house of bloodshed for having killed the Gibeonites" (II Sam. 21:1). Furthermore, the prophet narrator clearly condemns Saul for having "hunted them down in his zeal for the people of Israel and Judah" (II Sam. 21:2). Even the Gibeonites describe Saul as "a man who massacred us and who plotted against us... we have been wiped out from existence throughout Israel's borders" (II Sam. 21:5). Clearly, they view the former king's actions as a deliberate, premeditated purge that prevented them from living peacefully in the land.

Ralbag suggests that Saul annuls Joshua's agreement with the Gibeonites because, in his estimation, it is an accord created under false pretenses that makes Israel appear foolish.[2] His motivation is to reassert the nation's preeminence. By contrast, Abrabanel, commenting on the same verse, rejects this idea because the treaty was made over four hundred years earlier; it seems absurd to change the status quo after such a long time. Rabbi Amnon Bazak hypothesizes that when Saul clears the land of witchcraft (I Sam. 28:3), he decides to remove all foreign influences, including the Gibeonites, who may be practitioners of the dark arts.[3]

The simplest explanation is that King Saul, whose family is from Gibeon (a major religious site due to the presence of Tabernacle),[4] clashed with the locals.[5] Whatever the pretext, it appears that prior to King Saul's rule, the Gibeonites are secure, but during his reign they no longer have the protection of the authorities and are therefore an easy target.

Retribution

God reveals to King David that the famine is a punishment for Saul's conduct concerning the Gibeonites (II Sam. 21:3). The king then asks the

2. Ralbag on II Samuel 21:1.
3. Rabbi Amnon Bazak, "David and the Giv'onites," lecture no. 103, available at: http://www.hatanakh.com/sites/herzog/files/herzog/104.pdf.
4. See I Chronicles 8:29–33. Gibeon is a city in the territory of the tribe of Benjamin; it is given to the priests.
5. *Daat Mikra* on II Samuel 21:2 [Hebrew] (Mossad HaRav Kook), 502.

Gibeonites how Israel can atone for Saul's transgression. The Gibeonites reject monetary compensation and say that they have no quarrel with the Israelites, but as Saul is no longer alive, they request that David hand over seven of his sons for them to impale at Gibeah of Saul (II Sam. 21:6).

Why do they request exactly seven of Saul's children? According to the Talmud Yerushalmi, when Saul killed the priests in Nob, he harmed precisely seven Gibeonites: two woodcutters, two water carriers, a sexton, a cantor, and a scribe (Y. Kiddushin 4:1). This interpretation simply turns the situation into an act of direct revenge, an "eye for an eye," but the description of the original offense gives us the impression that Saul's actions are far more egregious. It is possible that these seven are the last remaining descendants of Saul. Alternatively, perhaps this is a play on the word *shevua*, "treaty," which is similar to the word *sheva*, "seven." With this reasoning, the request for seven sons hints that the Gibeonites are upholding the treaty that was broken by Saul.[6]

David tries to convince them to accept financial compensation (Y. Kiddushin 4:1). In verse 2, a seemingly parenthetical point is raised: the Gibeonites are not Israelites. The Gemara derives from here that Jews have three inherent traits: mercifulness, reticence, and kindness. The Gemara concludes that if one finds a Jew missing these traits, his lineage should be questioned (Yevamot 78b). The text highlights the fact that they are not Israelites in order to highlight the Gibeonites' decidedly non-Jewish, vengeful behavior which runs counter to the core values of the Jewish people.

Analysis

David is faced with a difficult and painful dilemma: Should he honor the Gibeonites' cruel demand, or reject it and try an alternative method to mollify the Gibeonites in order to stave off the famine's deadly effects? He chooses the first option. There is no harsh judgment given in the text regarding David's choice.[7] Modern scholarship explains that,

6. Rabbi Bazak, "David and the Giv'onites," available at: http://www.hatanakh.com/sites/herzog/files/herzog/104.pdf.
7. This is not the case in II Samuel 11:27, where the verse states: "And David's actions

serendipitously, this is a perfect way for David to rid himself of any claims to the throne.[8] Technically, however, none of these offspring could have ascended to the throne. The sons of a daughter are not eligible for the monarchy,[9] and neither are the sons of concubines.[10]

Once David begins negotiating with the Gibeonites, he has no recourse but to fulfill their request. Had he not consulted with the Gibeonites to begin with, he might have been able to prevent this tragedy, but as soon as he puts the ball in their court, he has to play by their rules. David accedes to their request and surrenders seven of Saul's sons: five sons of Merab and Adriel, who were raised by Michal,[11] and two sons of Rizpah, Saul's concubine. Merab's sons are referred to as Michal's children to teach us that even David's adopted sons aren't safe; although he must know them and probably loves them, he does not hesitate to sacrifice their lives.[12]

Rizpah bat Ayah's sons are named Armoni[13] and Mephibosheth. David has mercy on a grandson of Saul, a different Mephibosheth,[14] the handicapped son of Yonatan, with whom David had a covenant of eternal friendship (I Sam. 20:18, 42). If the famine is a result of a treaty breached by Saul, David's national duty is to honor the agreement despite his predecessor's laxity. Sparing Mephibosheth raises a moral quandary: Is it permissible to save one person knowing that another will be killed in his place?[15] The Gemara raises this issue and attempts to justify David's protection of Mephibosheth (Yevamot 78b). Here the narrative is expanded to suggest that David has Saul's descendants pass

---

were evil in the eyes of God."

8. See Joseph Blenkinsopp, *Gibeon and Israel: The Role of Gibeon and the Gibeonites in the Political and Religious History of Early Israel* (Cambridge University Press, 1972), 89–90 and Keith W. Whitelam, *The Just King: Monarchial Judicial Authority in Ancient Israel* (Sheffield: JSOT Press, 1979), 113, n. 50.
9. Maimonides, *Sefer Shofetim, Hilkhot Melakhim UMilḥemoteihem* 1:7.
10. *Daat Mikra* on II Samuel 21:7 [Hebrew] (Mossad HaRav Kook), 504.
11. Rashi on II Samuel 21:8.
12. *Shu"t Rashba* 1:10.
13. The name Armoni comes from the Hebrew word *armon*, "palace," as if to say "of the royal palace."
14. The name was common in Saul's family.
15. This question was posed to religious authorities during the Holocaust, who ruled that it was forbidden.

before the Holy Ark, with God choosing the victims. God's intervention in the process removes David from the equation and absolves him of any guilt. Since it is God's choice, David appeals to God on behalf of Mephibosheth and God accepts his supplication.

The surrender of Saul's offspring to be executed and publicly hanged for an extended period seems to contradict a number of biblical laws, including that of not killing sons for their father's crimes (Deut. 24:16) and not allowing a body to hang overnight, since that is disrespectful to God as man was made in His image (Deut. 21:23). In addition, are we permitted to turn over Jews to be summarily executed?[16] The Gemara's answer for these difficulties is that "it is better to uproot a letter of the Torah (i.e., transgress) than to publicly defile God's name" (Yevamot 7b). This means that the desecration of God's name that was caused by Saul's violation of the covenant (which was made in God's name) necessitated extraordinary measures to repair the breach, including disregarding – and even violating – biblical commands. A simple, if rather short-sighted, excuse is to say that as the punishment was meted out by the Gibeonites, the Jewish justice system is absolved of responsibility. Radak proposes that these descendants of Saul are guilty because they participated in the attacks on the Gibeonites. He rejects this approach, however, and offers an alternative explanation: while biblical commands constitute the directives that human courts must follow, God has His own justice system, different from human systems and therefore sometimes difficult for us to understand.[17] According to Maimonides, a king may use his discretion in ignoring biblical law in order to facilitate and maintain societal order.[18] In other words, in some instances, extraordinary circumstances warrant extraordinary behavior.

Ramifications

To atone for desecrating God's name, one must sanctify God's name.[19] Upon further investigation it is evident that this difficult episode did, in

16. Maimonides, *Sefer HaMadda, Hilkhot Yesodei HaTorah* 5:5.
17. Radak on II Samuel 21:1.
18. *Sefer Shofetim, Hilkhot Melakhim UMilḥemoteihem* 3:10.
19. Numbers Rabba 8.

fact, result in a sanctification of God's name. The Gemara relates that when passersby inquired about the hanging corpses, they were told that these were sons of the king who harmed converts, who were punished for their father's misdeeds. The people deduced that if even members of the royal family were subjected to capital punishment for their forebears' crimes, certainly ordinary people must respect and uphold their own commitments (Yevamot 78b). Furthermore, if this is the manner in which even quasi-converts are valued, how much more so should genuine converts be revered. This event led to the conversion of 150,000 people,[20] who eventually served as the laborers who helped King David's successor, Solomon, construct the Temple (I Kings 5:29).

A point to ponder is whether this seemingly positive outcome makes the entire episode more palatable.

Time Frame

The last few chapters of the book of Samuel are an appendix, and it is unclear when the events described in these chapters occur. There is no record of a famine during David's reign. Some suggest that this story takes place during the rebellion of Absalom.[21] When David flees Absalom, he meets a member of the tribe of Benjamin (from which Saul is descended), Shimei son of Gera. Shimei curses David, referring to him as the man with Saul's blood on his hands and the one responsible for the destruction of Saul's house (II Sam. 16:5–10). David never intended to harm Saul and even saves his life, so what is it that Shimei finds so reprehensible? It is plausible that he is referring to the incident in which King David surrenders Saul's descendants to the vengeful Gibeonites.

Act of Faith

In the Gemara cited above ("Ramifications") explaining that passersby are informed of the corpses that were hanged, we are not told the name

20. *Midrash Shmuel* 28.

21. *Daat Mikra* on II Samuel 21:1 [Hebrew] (Mossad HaRav Kook), 500.

of the person who reports these details. I would like to suggest that it was Rizpah.

The text tells us that this woman, mother of two of the deceased, builds a tent made of sackcloth adjacent to the gallows and stands guard over the bodies to protect them from the birds during the day and the animals at night (II Sam. 21:10). The corpses remain hanging for a full seven months, from the fifteenth of Nisan until the seventeenth of Ḥeshvan;[22] these are the scorching summer months of the Middle East, when the odor of the decaying corpses would have been the most offensive. When does she sleep? Eat? Bathe? Complain? Cry? Is this a form of silent protest? While the answers to these questions remain uncertain, it is clear that singlehandedly upholding the honor of the dead in this way was an enormous act of altruism and *ḥesed*, kindness.

Knowing that she is a fixture at the scene, it is logical to assume that she is the one disseminating information to curious onlookers. Despite being a widow whose two children have been killed, she does not appear to be bitter. In verse 10, the Midrash highlights the word *tzur*, meaning "rock," as the place upon which she encamps. The reason the text points out this seemingly trivial fact is because it is a word also used to refer to God.[23] In pitching her tent on the rock, Rizpah demonstrates her recognition that what has transpired is from Heaven and that she accepts the harsh divine judgment. In Biblical Hebrew, the name Rizpah means "burning coal."[24] Perhaps this reflects the message that with her exemplary act of faith, she successfully ignites the spark of God by inspiring passersby.

The prophet makes mention of her lineage; she is the daughter of Ayah. An *aya* is a non-kosher bird of prey known as a pernis.[25] It is not surprising that Rizpah is connected to an animal that attacks – this reflects her continuous protection of her children even after they have died. The pernis is a bird that has the ability to see great

---

22. Radak on II Samuel 21:11.
23. See Deuteronomy 32:4.
24. See I Kings 19 and Isaiah 10:6.
25. See Leviticus 11:14 and Deuteronomy 14:13.

distances, a trait also found in Rizpah, who can see beyond her personal anguish.

Conclusion

Rizpah's kindness to the deceased inspires King David to right another wrong. King Saul and his three sons had never received a proper burial after being killed at war with the Philistines, their bodies mockingly hung from the walls of the city Beit She'an (I Sam. 31). In this story, the Jews living in the town of Jabesh-Gilead slip in under cover of darkness, recover the bodies, and give them a secret burial. Having learned from Rizpah's actions, David collects the remains of Saul, Jonathan, and the sons left hanging, and reinters them in the family plot, affording them a proper state burial.[26] When God responds to David that the famine is because of Saul (Yevamot 78b), it is clear that the famine is not only a punishment for Saul reneging on a long-standing agreement but also for the fact that the nation had never given him the respect he deserved in death.

Once the Gibeonites are appeased and Saul is properly buried, the rains come and the famine ends.

Rizpah seems to be an incidental character in the narrative, but a closer study shows that she is the one who precipitates salvation. Although she is Saul's concubine rather than his wife, her name is revealed because she ultimately restores his honor in returning him to where he belongs, as well as protecting her children from harm even after their deaths. She is able to turn the terrible desecration of God's name into sanctification.

In Sophocles's play, there seemed to be no way for the sister to reconcile the king's command with the higher moral code. Rizpah, however, finds a way to follow the king's law even while protesting against it and maintaining the dignity of the deceased. *Antigone* ends in tragedy, leading to many more deaths. What would have happened had David said no to the Gibeonites? Would it have caused a civil war? And if Rizpah had not accepted the decree but incited people against the king, would more people have died?

---

26. Numbers Rabba 8.

Chapter 12

Athaliah

In the annals of history, it is not unusual to find family members who murder their relatives for political purposes. Cleopatra killed her sister Arsinoe IV and probably both of her brother-husbands. Herod assassinated his wife Mariamne and her children Alexander and Aristobolus IV, while Queen Didda of Kashmir murdered her three grandsons to consolidate her power. In modern times, the 2017 brutal elimination of Kim Jong-nam is widely believed to have been perpetrated at the behest of his half-brother Kim Jong Un as a vicious attempt by the North Korean leader to solidify his position as ruler.

In approximately 850 BCE, Athaliah, the queen of Judea, earned the dubious distinction of being the most dramatic murderer of family members in the Bible.

Background

Ahab serves as king of Israel for twenty-two years (I Kings 16:29). He marries Jezebel, a princess from Sidon (I Kings 16:31), who has a negative influence on the king (I Kings 21:25). The monarchs' evil nature leads the prophet Elijah to curse them and prophesy destruction and dishonorable death for the king and his descendants (I Kings 21:17–28). Ahab indeed succumbs to his battle wounds (I Kings 22:35). He is succeeded by his son, Ahaziah, who rules for two years and follows in his father's evil footsteps (I Kings 22:52–53). His brief reign ends with his early death, in fulfillment of Elijah's prophecy (II Kings 1:17).

Following his passing, the childless Ahaziah's brother Joram inherits the throne (II Kings 1:17). In Joram's fifth year as king of Israel, Jehoram son of Jehoshaphat is crowned king of Judea and marries Ahab's daughter, Athaliah. Thus, the kings of the divided nation of Israel are brothers-in-law: Athaliah's brother Joram is king of Israel and her husband Jehoram is king of Judah (II Kings 8:18).

Athaliah's husband, Jehoram, dies and their son, Ahaziah, is installed as the new king of Judea (II Kings 8:25). When his uncle, his mother's brother Joram, is wounded in battle and begins recuperating in the Jezreel Valley, Ahaziah decides to visit him to check on his welfare.

Meanwhile, Elijah's successor, Elisha, secretly appoints the non-royal Jehu as the new king of Israel, usurping Joram. He is charged with wiping out Ahab's royal dynasty (II Kings 9:1–10) and reestablishing genuine worship of God.

Jehu travels to Jezreel, where he kills both Joram the son of Ahab and Ahaziah, the maternal grandson of Ahab (II Kings 9:24–28). Jehu then kills Jezebel, queen mother of Israel (II Kings 9:33) along with another seventy sons of Ahab (II Kings 10:7). Jehu continues to eradicate an additional forty-two descendants of Ahab, in fulfillment of Elijah's curse (II Kings 10:14). When Ahab succumbs to his battle wounds, the Kingdom of Israel is free of Ahab's progeny and Jehu begins a new dynasty.

Roots of Evil

The first time Athaliah is mentioned in the Bible is when she marries Jehoram, son of Jehoshaphat. Her name probably comes from the root A-T-L, which means bravery in the ancient Akkadian language. Athaliah summarily asserts her negative influence over her new husband, the king. Jehoram dies eight years into his reign and is succeeded by his son Ahaziah.

Athaliah is referred to as the "daughter of Omri" (II Kings 8:26), who the Bible describes as the most evil person to exist until that point (I

Kings 16:25). It is interesting that the text identifies her as the daughter of Omri when, in fact, she was the daughter of Omri's son Ahab. While it is unusual to associate a character with their grandparent rather than their parent, it does occasionally happen in the biblical narrative.[1] Perhaps the narrator's intention is to make very clear the connection between Athaliah and the evil dynasty of Omri. *Daat Mikra* speculates that the purpose of tracing her lineage to Omri is to emphasize that Athaliah is not a product of the union between Ahab and the gentile Jezebel.[2] Rather, she was the daughter of one of Ahab's Jewish wives, which means that when she marries into the southern kingdom, the purity of the House of David is maintained.[3]

The Purge

Shockingly and inexplicably, Athaliah reacts to the news of her son Ahaziah's death by executing all her male grandsons, the potential heirs to the throne, and installing herself as the sole Judean monarch. Athaliah's reign lasts six years.

What could have caused Athaliah to destroy all the possible heirs to the throne? One possibility is that the deaths of her son, brother, mother, and all her male relatives trigger a mental collapse, a tragic case of overwhelming, catastrophic news translating into a psychotic fit of lunacy that includes illogical and barbarous behavior. The difficulty with this approach is that it undermines the likelihood of Athaliah successfully navigating her position after eliminating her progeny. If the devastating episode led to mental instability, it is hard to fathom that she would be capable of deftly managing the affairs of state for six years.[4] On the

1. See Yevamot 62b.
2. *Daat Mikra* on II Kings 8:26 [Hebrew] (Mossad HaRav Kook), 557.
3. This would explain a significant issue. Jezebel is clearly a non-Jew, as would be her children. In the Kingdom of Israel this apparently didn't bother anyone, but in the Judean kingdom, bloodlines were more important. A descendant from the Judean line of David would have had to marry a Jew, and so Athaliah cannot be a daughter of Jezebel.
4. Though such a scenario seems unlikely, we do know of a number of monarchs who

other hand, if her breakdown was only a case of "temporary insanity," her tenure as queen would be easier to comprehend.

Alternatively, Rabbi Adin Steinsaltz suggests that Athaliah has only one ambition: to rule.[5] This desire is so powerful that she is relentlessly driven to do all that is necessary to accomplish this goal. Athaliah is not described as mentally challenged or crazed, but as "the evil one" (II Chr. 24:7.) She has an unwavering, voracious appetite for power. Her actions are determined, calculated and cold-blooded. Despite the obvious fact that by massacring all her progeny she unequivocally ensures that a monarchal dynasty would never appear, she proceeds with her nefarious intentions.

Another possibility is that this is a strategic maneuver to save the Kingdom of Judah and her own life, since it is uncertain whether Jehu would have attacked the Kingdom of Judah after successfully eliminating the Kingdom of Israel. If Jehu had attacked the Kingdom of Israel, perhaps a full-blown civil war would have ensued. By eliminating her male descendants, Athaliah does the bloody work for him, making it unlikely that Jehu would wage war just to subdue a woman (whom he undoubtedly views as far less threatening).[6] Athaliah's extreme actions were an effort to stave off the marauding Jehu, protect herself, and preserve the autonomy of the kingdom. The weakness of this argument lies in the fact that Jehu does not seem to have any qualms about assassinating women – he has already murdered Jezebel, Ahab's wife. Athaliah's assessment that he would refrain from attacking women is baseless.

Another possible way to decipher the puzzle of Athaliah's motives is to say that she wanted revenge. While harming Jehu was beyond her reach, she could repudiate and rebel against what he represented: the abolishment of false deities and the return to the Jewish faith. Athaliah's misguided, violent response of eradicating the remnants of the Davidic line was aimed at putting an end to the purity of faith that is crucial in

---

lived with mental illness, including Henry VI of England, George III of England, and Otto of Bavaria.

5. Rabbi Adin Steinsaltz, *Biblical Women* (Tel Aviv: Misrad HaBitaḥon, 1983), 84.
6. *Daat Mikra* on II Kings [Hebrew] (Mossad HaRav Kook), 591.

fostering a connection between God and the Jewish nation.[7] Josephus explains that "she endeavored that none of the House of David might be left alive; but that the whole family might be exterminated: that no king might arise out of it afterward."[8]

According to Josephus, Herod commanded his servants that, upon his death, a large number of distinguished people should be murdered so that the entire nation would mourn and there would be public expressions of grief.[9] Similarly, Athaliah wants her subjects to grieve as she weeps over the decimated house of Ahab. And indeed, she provides them with good reason to mourn.

Queen

Athaliah rules for six years. This somewhat lengthy reign indicates a measure of stability and acceptance by her subjects. Perhaps as wife and mother of the king, she is familiar with the royal duties involved in the successful administration of the kingdom. In addition, government officials are already accustomed to obeying her, and so now, following the upheaval in the palace, they simply continue to carry out her orders. This isn't a substantive departure from the past, but a continuation, with Athaliah assuming an expanded role. The Judean kingdom enjoys a stable monarchy with orderly succession from father to son. This lies in stark contrast to the Kingdom of Israel, which is rife with palace coups and political upheavals.[10] Although the text does not specify which political and military factions back Athaliah, it is clear that she has wide popular support.[11] Athaliah has so much confidence in her standing that she ignores the threatening noises. When she hears a commotion, she doesn't entertain the thought that a rebellion is afoot (II Kings 11:13).

An unusual spelling of Athaliah's name in the text, with an additional letter changing it to Athaliahu, leads to a surprising comment from

7. Rabbi Yigal Ariel, *Mikdash Melekh* [Hebrew] (Hispin: Midrash HaGolan, 1994), 319.
8. Josephus, *Antiquities of the Jews* 9:7:1.
9. Ibid., 17:6:5.
10. Rabbi Adin Steinsaltz, *Biblical Women* (Tel Aviv: Misrad HaBitaḥon, 1983), 81.
11. See II Kings 11:4. Jehoiada doesn't just present a new king, he sets up security.

Rashi. He explains that the extra letter, *vav*, is added to her name as an accolade because she was a "woman of valor."[12] It is astonishing that Rashi describes a mass murderer as a praiseworthy person. Perhaps she deserves some sort of recognition because of her success as a monarch.

The scant account of Athaliah's reign chronicles the damage she causes to the Temple (II Chr. 24:7), the service she impedes there,[13] and the priestly service schedule that is cancelled.[14]

It is worth pointing out that there is considerable halakhic difficulty with a woman serving as the leader of the Jewish people. The fact that Athaliah seizes power rather than being appointed may serve as a mitigating factor that allows her tenure to stand unchallenged.[15]

Like Mother, Like Daughter

Although it remains an open question whether Athaliah is Jezebel's biological daughter, she is certainly her ideological heir. Athaliah constructs temples devoted to idolatry in Jerusalem (II Kings 11:18), just as Jezebel did years earlier in the region of Samaria (I Kings 16:32). Both influence their families negatively and have no moral reservations about eliminating anyone they view as a threat. Jezebel manipulates her husband Ahab and proves to be the dominant personality in that relationship. Similarly, Athaliah seizes power and rules forcefully as queen. While both women are murdered, Jezebel dies as an elegant, dignified queen with her imperial clothing and makeup in place, while Athaliah ignobly rips her royal garments when she realizes that she has been ousted.

Joash

Ironically, Athaliah kills only her male descendants because she does not see the females as viable challenges to her authority. King Joram's daughter, Jehosheba, rescues a child, Joash, from Athaliah's killing spree.

---

12. Rashi on II Chronicles 13:2.
13. *Yalkut Shimoni* on *Naso*, 714.
14. Rashi on II Kings 11:18.
15. Maimonides, *Sefer Shofetim, Hilkhot Melakhim UMilḥemoteihem* 1:6.

Joash is secretly held in protective custody for six years by Jehosheba and her husband, the high priest Jehoiada, along with a group of priestly co-conspirators.[16]

It is said that Joash was ensconced somewhere in the Temple, either in the attic, basement, dormitory, linen closet, or perhaps even inside the Holy of Holies.[17]

Conclusion

When Joash reaches the age of seven, Jehoiada publicizes Joash's unlikely survival beyond his small circle of accomplices and arranges a carefully organized and heavily secured coronation ceremony in the Temple court. Jehoiada places the crown of David upon Joash's head, and the crowd accepts his authority, crying out "Long live the king!" (II Kings 11:12). Upon hearing the commotion, Athaliah rushes out to investigate and witnesses the inauguration of the new king and the raucous, joyous celebration. She rips her royal garments and speaks for the first time in the narrative, shrieking: "Rebellion! Rebellion!" It appears that she is totally blindsided by the swift turn of events.

Her desperate cries and the tearing of her garments reflect the deposed queen's abrupt state of mourning. What is less clear is the exact source of her grief. She could, of course, be mourning the collapse of her monarchy, but perhaps, having seen that a child has survived and that consequently, the murders she committed six years earlier were for naught, she is mourning the meaningless deaths of her grandchildren.

---

16. This is not the first time we have a successful union between a member of the tribe of Judah and a member of the tribe of Levi: Aaron (tribe of Levi) married Elisheva (tribe of Judah).
17. See Rashi and Radak on II Kings 11:2.

Sherri's Story: The Blessing of a Broken Heart

By Sherri Mandell

Koby Mandell and his friend Yosef Ishran were brutally stoned to death by Palestinian terrorists on May 8, 2001, in a cave near their home in Tekoa. Koby's mother Sherri shares her painful struggle to make sense of the tragedy. These excerpts from her book, *The Blessing of a Broken Heart* (The Toby Press), are reprinted with the permission of the publisher.

My thirteen-year-old son Koby entered the cave – but he did not emerge. I thought my family and I would be lost in a cave of grief, forever wandering in a labyrinth so dark you can't even see your own hand, but have to trust that when you step, the ground will still be under you. I could have stayed in bed the rest of my life mourning him. I could have remained broken, resenting my life, my lot. But there is something in me that refuses to be broken, no matter how intense the pain, something that moves toward the light.

Mourning my son has similarities to labor. The contractions of pain rush through my body like a knot that is tied tighter and tighter so that I am unable to breathe, dead along with my son…. It feels like I am pregnant, pregnant with death, giving birth to a new self – a self that can navigate the depths of suffering and yet go on with life.

I falter at times. I fall into grief. I despair at meaning. What is meaning with my son gone? And then the wave of pain passes. I swim toward his life and death, reaching again for meaning, a raft that will keep me from drowning.

A mother should not have to watch her son being put into the ground. A mother should die before her child. A mother should not have to bear witness to the terrible fact that much as she loves her child, she can't protect him.

"What do we do with this pain?" my husband asks a rabbi who, years ago, lost an eleven-year-old child in a bus accident. The rabbi answers: "You must use it to grow."

Because no matter how much we try to intellectualize or interpret the pain, to will it away, the pain crouches on our hearts like a beast who is waiting to crush us, to chew us to bits until we are nothing, dust that the wind can blow away.

I was surprised when I found out that the halakhic (traditional) Jewish period for mourning a child is only thirty days. But one of the grieving mothers explained why: It's because you grieve the rest of your life. You don't need rituals to remind you to grieve. You will think of your child forever.

I have to live with the contradictions of my son's death – the suffering I experience in the midst of an outpouring of love and support; a son who is alive in my mind and dead at the same time; my need to live in this world and reach toward the world to come; the terrible beauty of the place that he was killed.

Every parent who loses a child feels guilty, no matter how the child dies. Cancer, kidney failure, drowning, fire – there is something the parent feels he could have done to prevent the death. There is pain, and then there is guilt. You can recover from the pain, but guilt can eat you every day like acid.

It's okay to cry, to be sad. Accepting my pain means that I don't have to be afraid of it. Neither do my children or husband. The pain sometimes feels like panic and fear, like madness. But if you can find a way to let it live, you can bear it without being broken. Then you can begin to heal, sewing your life back together one stitch at a time.

I feel sorry for the pain my children already know. A newspaper reporter from Scotland tells me she feels sorry for my children. I tell her there's a lot to feel sorry for. But maybe this tragedy will make them into even greater people with bigger hearts and wide-open eyes. Maybe if I show them we can live with the tragedy, so we make more of our lives, well then, maybe his death won't just hurt them, but will help them too. They already know the worst life has to offer. They have seen the evil in the world: they know how death lurks behind everything. To have such knowledge at such a young age could mean they can go forth as agents of blessing in this world....

The pain of mourning is so intense that you wish that you could die. It's a pain that you don't think you can bear, but you can bear it.... Pain is like carrying a heavy barbell in your backpack. You can't go as freely as you used to. But the more you carry it, the stronger you get.

My job is not to forgive – but to give meaning. My job is to remember.

Koby's murder is a robbery, an amputation, and a rape. I stand naked, battered. The pain we feel is extraordinarily powerful and overwhelming. But the pain can either push a person into a spiral of depression or be an impetus and a spur for growth. It depends on how we handle it.

Not an hour goes by that he is not in my head and heart. Every morning I rise to his death and every evening I go to sleep with it. The trick is to forbid death to be more present than life, not to forsake my life and my other children for the memory of all that I have lost.

We don't see what's inside of people. Inside of almost everyone is a pocket of pain – some pockets are bigger, some are smaller – but they are always there.

Each day, I have to work to go on; each day I decide to live. I am not the same person as I was. That is the way it should be. Losing Koby means part of me was killed. But rather than mourn the person I was, I work to bless the person I have become....

I have learned that everything, even the worst trial, contains sparks of holiness and it is up to us to release those sparks and bring them into the world.

I do not bless the bad. But I understand that light comes from darkness, and that evil exists in the world so that we can choose to do good. Evil exists to be conquered....

We humans can only use vessels if they are unbroken; we can't put a broken pail into the well and drink. Yet it is when our hearts are broken that God sculpts our souls, prodding open the narrow entrances to the caves of our being. Whenever God takes from you, He has to give you something back. God has given me the blessing of a broken heart.

Sherri Mandell is a prize-winning author whose latest book is *The Kabbalah of Writing: Mystical Practices for Inspiration and Creativity.* She lives in Israel with her family.

Part Four

Women Whose Children Play a Role in the Salvation of the World

והוא יחל להושיע

(Judges 13:5)

Chapter 13

Daughters of Lot

The idea that unsavory actions are at times necessary to achieve desired outcomes is attributed to Machiavelli. However, this presumption is complex, and it leads to challenging questions and situations. Who determines which actions are justified by their results, and how do they do that? For example, is it always legitimate to risk soldiers' lives by sending them into battle? How does a physician weigh the consequences of amputating a limb in order to save a patient's life? If the conductor of a runaway train is faced with the dilemma of either choosing a direction which will almost definitely kill one of the passengers, or a different direction regarding which there is a lesser possibility, but a possibility nonetheless, that ten people may die, what should he do? Is it appropriate to lie in order to help a promising couple begin courting? Is stealing ever justified – what about stealing medicine to save a person's life? Is the targeted killing of a fearsome terrorist appropriate if it prevents future civilian casualties? Is detonating a nuclear warhead, which will undoubtedly cause great harm to innocents, the correct course of action if it leads to ending a world war and preventing an endless number of deaths?

Not all of these scenarios have unequivocal solutions, and sometimes the solution feels uncomfortable. Genesis 19 describes a curious dilemma that the daughters of Lot face and the bizarre decision that they choose, undoubtedly justifying their deed with a firm view of the end result.

Background

Following Abraham's circumcision (Gen. 18), three angels dressed as men come to his tent to heal him, to inform him that Sarah will bear a son, and to destroy Sodom.[1] God tells Abraham that His intent to obliterate the city is a result of its inhabitants' sinful ways, and Abraham bargains with God to save it.

Two of the angels[2] arrive in Sodom (Gen. 19:1) – one to save Abraham's nephew Lot and his family, and the other to destroy the city. Each angel has a specific job to accomplish, as does every human being. They arrive in the evening in order to leave time for Abraham to pray for the city to be spared. Lot greets them at the entrance to the city and invites them into his home.[3] He does not run to greet them, nor does he prostrate himself in the way that Abraham did, but he does serve them a feast, including matza, like Abraham. The guests initially refuse his invitation but ultimately accede to his pressure. Lot passes the test established for him.

Immediately upon their arrival, the whole town (Gen. 19:4), old and young, forms an unruly mob and surrounds the house, demanding that Lot surrender the guests so that they can abuse them. This was their way of enforcing the "anti-immigration laws" that they viewed as imperative for the survival of their wealthy, lush society. If guests were routinely harmed in Sodom, they would naturally stay away.[4]

1. Rashi on Genesis 18:2.
2. Compared to Abraham, they are regular people, but in Sodom they are clearly angels.
3. Comparing the hospitality of Lot to that of Abraham, we find that Abraham has his guests wash their dusty feet before entering his tent, as dust was part of their idol worship. He was willing to accept them into his home, but he would not accept their beliefs. Lot, on the other hand, isn't bothered by his guests' idol worship. In fact, he does not want them to wash up – if the townspeople discover them in his home, he wants it to appear as if they have just arrived.
4. How then does Lot relocate to Sodom? It seems that he was accepted because of his wealth and prestigious lineage – he is the nephew of Abraham, who saved Sodom from the four kings.

Good Intentions

In order to protect his guests, Lot approaches the crowd and begs them to refrain from their evil intentions (Gen. 19:7). Harming his visitors is an unconscionable act of malevolence that Lot finds intolerable. He attempts to quench the rowdy crowd's carnal thirst by presenting his two virgin daughters as alternatives. It seems that Lot does not consider this evil behavior, and that abuse of women is apparently of little concern to him. His intention is to save his heavenly guests, but his means of achieving their salvation – allowing his daughters to be sexually assaulted – is highly questionable. Nahmanides points out that most men would rather kill or be killed than allow the women of their family to be molested, yet Lot offers his daughters on his own initiative.[5] In order to establish a safe place for the guests, he places his daughters in danger, teaching his daughters that violating another person is not necessarily evil if it is for a reasonable cause – an important point for later in the story. Lot tries to perform an act of kindness, but it is a twisted, broken form.

Sforno tries to mitigate Lot's perversion by suggesting that these two daughters were engaged to be married to men from Sodom, and Lot expected these men to come to the defense of their fiancées.[6]

Despite Lot's perverted sense of morality, there is reason to save him: he showed mercy to the guests he graciously hosted, and so God has mercy on him. This trait was likely learned in the house of Abraham, whose merit may also serve as protection here. When Abraham negotiates with God on behalf of Sodom, he begins by asking God to spare the city if fifty righteous people can be found, but as he lowers the number and continues to plead for clemency for Sodom, he never dips below ten. Abraham assumes there are ten worthy people in Lot's household: Lot, his wife, their four daughters, and the daughters' husbands.

According to the Gemara (Sanhedrin 109b), Lot had a fifth daughter who was executed for feeding a traveler. She violated Sodom's strict laws by providing aid to the downtrodden, and the city's criminal justice

---

5. Nahmanides on Genesis 19:8.
6. Sforno on Genesis 19:8.

system made an example of her to deter others from duplicating this crime. Interestingly, despite raising his children in an environment that is the polar opposite of his uncle Abraham's home, Lot inculcates the next generation with Abraham's teachings.

In this chapter, Lot is portrayed as a problematic figure who has good intentions but uses morally questionable means to accomplish his goals. To his credit, he maintains some of the lessons that he learned from Abraham and transmits them to his children.

Escape

The angels take control of the situation and instruct Lot to take his family and leave the city. His Sodomite sons-in-law scoff at Lot's "the end is near" harangue, refusing to believe his warning (Gen. 19:14). The angels literally take the family by the hand (Gen. 19:15) and force them to escape, commanding them not to look back so as to make a total break with their past in order to strive forward.

Lot's wife, Irit, turns to observe the carnage and is transformed into a pillar of salt. She is punished for violating the angels' clear injunction and not being able to completely sever herself from the evil society that she was fleeing. While the possibility exists that she turned to see whether her remaining daughters were following behind, the fact that she was subjected to such a severe punishment suggests that it was more likely that she still felt connected to her hometown and its lifestyle. She was subjected to this odd form of death in retribution for asking her neighbors for salt, as it alerted the town that guests had arrived and led to the consequences that followed.

Lot's flight from Sodom is reminiscent of the Exodus from Egypt:[7] Lot serves matza to his guests, reminding us of the matza the Jews ate in Egypt. He is outside the house pleading with his neighbors on behalf of the angels while the family shelters behind closed doors, just as the Jews in Egypt ate the paschal lamb securely protected in their homes while God eliminated Egypt's firstborn. The angels smite the hostile horde

7. Rabbi Yaakov Medan, *The Word is Very Near* [Hebrew] (Tel Aviv: Yedioth Books, 2014), 133.

with blindness and implore the family to leave Sodom quickly, just as the Jewish slaves left Egypt in a hurry. Lot carries within him the seed of Israel's ultimate redeemer, and therefore his redemption shares elements of the nation's redemption.

Trauma and Response

Lot and his remaining two daughters are understandably in a state of shock and trauma. Within a matter of hours, their wife/mother, daughters/sisters, finances, home, and neighbors have all vanished. Life as they knew it has disappeared.

God initially intends to destroy all five boroughs of Sodom, but Lot requests to be allowed to move to the smallest city, Zoar, and God complies. After a short while, however, Lot leaves with his two daughters and settles in a cave: "Lot went up from Zoar and settled in the hills together with his two daughters because he was afraid to stay in Zoar. He and his two daughters settled in a cave" (Gen. 19:30). In this verse, Lot and his daughters are mentioned twice: at the beginning, where Lot's fear is highlighted, and at the end, after they relocate to the cave. It is odd that the source of Lot's fear is omitted. If his fear is based on the uncomfortable interactions with the people of Zoar, then his retreat to a dark – and inherently frightening – cave is puzzling.

"The elder said to the younger, 'Our father is old, and there is no man left on earth to come to us in the normal way of the world. Let us get our father drunk with wine and then sleep with him, so that we may raise a new generation through our father'" (Gen. 19:32–33). The text does not inform the reader whether Lot is physically too old or too traumatized to participate and function in rebuilding the family. The daughters see their situation as a problem because "there is no man left on earth." According to Rashi (Gen. 19:31), these women believe that they are the last three remaining humans on the planet, akin to Noah's family who were the sole survivors of the Flood. Nahmanides says that the daughters assume that they bear sole responsibility for the continuity of the human species, and that is why they scheme to become pregnant from their father. They plan to do their part, hoping that God will grant one of them a male child and the other a female, thereby ensuring the world's survival.[8] If their motivation is sincere, we can say that their intentions are moral and even righteous, but their methodology is still questionable. Like their misguided father, they want to perform a selfless act of kindness, but its form is broken.

One wonders why they would presume that they are the only survivors. Following their escape from Sodom, they have undoubtedly met the inhabitants of Zoar who avoided the devastation. They are also certainly aware of the presence of Abraham's family. It would be reasonable for them to surmise that the destruction was limited to Sodom, and that Abraham's family is unaffected. Had they been forthright and truly righteous, they would have informed Lot of their suspicions, rather than ply him with alcohol and trick him into fulfilling his role in their deception.

Nahmanides explains that even though father-daughter cohabitation is not technically forbidden under the seven Noahide laws, incest has always been an unseemly liaison frowned upon by all societies, and Lot's daughters are uncomfortable discussing the matter with him for that reason. As we have seen, it was their father who taught them back in Sodom that in extreme circumstances, sexually deviant acts are acceptable. One cannot imagine that they would have considered such a plan otherwise.

Sforno argues that the daughters realize there are other people in the world, but because they are caring for their aging father, they aren't able to go search for them.[9] Radak suggests that they are aware that others exist, but they are concerned that since they are from Sodom, no one will want to marry them lest the destruction follow them. Conversely, the *Daat Zekenim* proposes that because these women have been saved, they view themselves as special, on a higher level; they feel that no commoner would be worthy of marrying them. The perspective of these commentators removes any noble element of the daughters' decision. Instead, they view their motivation as self-centered and egotistical. There is no altruism here.

An alternative approach, which defends the daughters' intentions as honorable and based on *ḥesed*, is the suggestion that they are aware of

8. Nahmanides on Genesis 19:32.
9. Sforno on Genesis 19:32.

the biblical law of *yibum*. Under this law, if a man dies childless, a close male relative is obliged to marry his widow and give some form of continuity to the ancestral line of the deceased. The underlying purpose of this command is to do a kindness for the dead, as the child of this union would inherit the deceased's name and property. Lot's daughters realize that the family's gene pool is reaching its conclusion, and they want to leave behind offspring as an act of benevolence.

The women need to ply their father with wine to successfully implement their incestuous plan. One may wonder where they find the wine, though the presence of wine in a cave is not surprising, as in ancient times it was common practice to age wine in cool, dark caves. Rashi, however, sees the chance discovery of wine in the cave as proof of divine intervention in the enterprises of man. God does not provide the women with explicit instructions as to what course of action to take, but by placing the wine at their ready disposal, He was indirectly, yet crucially, involved in the execution of their scheme, which ultimately facilitated the birth of two large nations.

The older daughter is the one to hatch the scheme. Interestingly, she is referred to as the *beḥira*, although she isn't the firstborn; we know of older, married daughters of Lot who stayed behind in Sodom.[10] This term is used in order to further underscore the connection to the Egyptian redemption and the role of the firstborn.

On the first night, the older daughter sleeps with Lot, and the following night, the younger daughter repeats the act. Lot himself is unaware of what has transpired. Miraculously, both daughters become pregnant. Their plan is to produce one female and one male offspring in order to prevent the extinction of the human race (or perhaps just the extinction of their family), but they both bear boys, who eventually blossom into the large nations of Moab and Ammon. Both Abraham and Lot welcome guests into their homes, and both are rewarded with children who give birth to nations.

While the text does not condemn the daughters' incestuous deed, Lot, the unwitting participant, disappears from the narrative after this

---

10. In Genesis 19:14, Lot goes to his sons-in-law and tells them to leave. They laugh at him.

humiliating experience. Abraham distances himself from his nephew to disassociate himself from Lot.[11]

It appears that being impaired as a result of excessive alcohol consumption may be the reason for committing a crime, but it is not an excuse. The daughters learned their behavior from their father – just as he protected his guests through an immoral deed, so his daughters gallantly try to save humanity through immoral behavior. Nahmanides points out that as soon as he offered up his daughters for abuse as a bargaining chip to the rowdy mob in Sodom, he paved the way for his daughters to abuse him, since it was easy to surmise from Lot's behavior that molestation was not forbidden or even considered a negative act.

In the biblical text, we find *puncta extraordinaria*[12] above the Hebrew word *uvkuma*, "and when she woke up." Rashi explains that this extra dot above the second *vav* indicates that when Lot wakes up on the morning after the first night, he knows what has transpired, and yet he allows himself to become drunk again on the second night. Rashi is critical of Lot and portrays him as a misguided person whose obscene gesture in Sodom shifts his family toward deviant sexual behavior; since he models this kind of behavior, he is ultimately responsible for the brief incestuous affair that happens later. Lot also rejects the angels' instruction to return to Abraham, a move which would have prevented this unfortunate incident from ever occurring.[13]

The text repeats the story of each daughter's encounter with their father. It could have simply stated, "and the younger went and slept with him."[14] Why was it necessary to chronicle the squalid details twice? Clearly, the text heaps further humiliation on Lot for his seedy behavior, but it also subtly decries the older daughter's actions compared to her younger sister. Not only is all of this the older daughter's idea, but the younger one also displays a certain degree of modesty.[15] The older

11. *Midrash Aggada* on Genesis 20:1.
12. In ancient texts of the Bible, dots (known today as *puncta extraordinaria*) were occasionally inserted above certain words to attenuate the strict meaning of the word. See Genesis 33:4 for another example, and see Rashi there for an explanation.
13. Rashi on Genesis 19:17–19.
14. See Genesis 32:19 for an example of this style in the biblical text.
15. The verse says explicitly that the older daughter "came and lay with her father,"

daughter names her child Moab, literally, "from my father," publicly proclaiming the sordid liaison.[16] The younger daughter uses more subtle language, calling her child Ben Ami, "the son of my nation," nowhere near as glaring a reference to the baby's paternity. Perhaps the use of the terms "firstborn" and "younger" to identify the sisters reflects the theme of many stories in Genesis in which the younger sibling is in some way superior to the one who was born first.

The Jewish people were destined to have a complicated relationship with these two nations in future generations. The Israelites are proscribed from warring with these nations (Deut. 2:9), reflecting a certain level of allegiance, while curiously, they are not accepted for conversion (Deut. 23:7) due to their continued twisted attitude toward *ḥesed*, indicating a certain level of enmity. These foreign nations do not allow the Israelites to pass through their land peacefully on their way to Israel following their forty-year sojourn in the desert, nor do they provide them with bread and water. On the advice of Balaam, however, they send their daughters to seduce the Jewish men and cause them to sin.

Two important personalities descend from the union of Lot and his daughters. Ruth, the direct ancestor of King David, is a Moabite convert and a descendant of Lot's older daughter. Naamah, the wife of Solomon and the mother of King Rehoboam, is a descendant of Lot's younger daughter. According to kabbalistic sources, Ruth is a reincarnation of the older daughter, and she rectifies her ancestor's distorted *ḥesed* when she reveals her identity to Boaz.[17]

The *Shem MiShmuel* argues that it was God's plan for the Jewish monarchy to originate outside the Jewish gene pool.[18] Since Jews view themselves as equal brothers before the Lord, likened to a single body, it would be inappropriate for one among them to rule over the masses. The superiority of an individual, as is implicit in a monarchy, is the antithesis of the Jewish worldview. For this reason, God introduces

---

whereas regarding the younger one, it says that she "arose and lay with him." Also see the names of the children.

16. Genesis Rabba 51:14.
17. Alsheikh, *Einei Moshe*, 3.
18. *Shem MiShmuel, Parashat Bemidbar,* Shavuot 1910.

the monarchy from outside the nation. Additionally, as the Messiah (who will come from the Davidic line) will be tasked with redeeming not only Jews but the entire world, a connection to the other nations will be both necessary and desirable.

A remarkable story appears in Rabbi Moshe Feinstein's halakhic responsa *Iggerot Moshe.*[19] This multi-volume publication is a heavy, classic Jewish legal text that is far from a storybook and does not delve into mysticism or supernatural events. Atypical for this work, Rabbi Feinstein tells a story that he personally experienced in his village in Europe: A parishioner was afflicted with a strange disease – macroglossia, an enlarged tongue. When Rabbi Feinstein visited him, the patient divulged the etiology of the illness. One week earlier, when the Torah portion was read in the synagogue – that week, it was *Parashat Vayera* – the man mocked and spoke disparagingly about the daughters of Lot. That night, two women with covered faces appeared to him in a dream and claimed that they came from the afterlife. They explained that they were the daughters of Lot, and since they had been miraculously saved and they were Abraham's relatives, they could have claimed that they became pregnant through immaculate conception and even established a new religion. Nonetheless, they purposely named their children Moab and Ammon, fully cognizant that doing so would subject them to millennia of ridicule, in order to dispel this notion and remind mankind that a child always has a father of flesh and blood, and any claim to the contrary is folly. For this, they are rewarded with being the maternal ancestors of the eventual Messiah.

Shortly thereafter, the man succumbed to his illness. Rabbi Feinstein offers this story as a proof text that there is no prohibition of *yiḥud* (being alone in a room together) between father and daughter.

---

19. *Iggerot Moshe, Even HaEzer* 4:64.

Chapter 14

Tamar, Daughter-in-Law of Judah

In the 1998 film *The Truman Show*, the protagonist, Truman, lives an ordinary, mundane existence, oblivious to the fact that his entire life is broadcast as an ongoing television series where viewers tune in to watch the drama unfold from a distance, and his "family and friends" are a cast of actors playing scripted roles. Eventually, Truman uncovers the reality of his circumstances and plots his escape.

The Midrash in Genesis 38 describes an eerily similar scenario.[1] The main characters may or may not be aware that they are effectively actors on God's world stage. Jacob's sons earnestly negotiate the sale of their brother, Jacob mourns the disappearance of Joseph, Reuben repents for his sin, and Judah is in the process of establishing a family while God sows the seeds of the final redemption.

Checking Out

The chapter begins by telling us: *Vayered Yehuda me'et eḥav*, literally, "Judah went down from his brothers" (Gen. 38:1). The family lives in the

1. Genesis Rabba 85:1.

city of Hebron, which is situated in a mountain range. Judah does indeed descend geographically, but he is also falling spiritually from his elevated status. It is unclear whether Judah is banished from his brethren or he willingly departs. Judah has rescued Joseph from certain death by proposing and initiating the fateful sale that would alter the destiny of Jewish history. But he could have done more. He wields sufficient influence among his brothers that had he demanded that no harm befall Joseph, they would have listened and Joseph would have returned home safely.[2] When the sons see the deep anguish that Joseph's disappearance causes their father, it is entirely possible that they blamed Judah for not exercising his influence and insisting that Joseph remain untouched. Being entangled in such a difficult situation leads to Judah's departure, either voluntarily or because the brothers compel him to do so.

Judah's descent and disassociation from his family leads him to act in ways that are antithetical to the conduct that would be appropriate for a descendant of such a moral, upstanding family. He befriends the locals (Gen. 38:1) and marries the daughter of a Canaanite, Shua (Gen. 38:2).[3] Earlier in Genesis, when Abraham sends Eliezer to find a wife for Isaac, he emphasizes that under no circumstances should Eliezer choose a Canaanite spouse (Gen. 24:3). Rebecca also tells Isaac that Jacob must leave Canaan to find a wife since the local women are not an appropriate match for him (Gen. 27:46). Now Judah ignores the family directive. If we take the view that Judah leaves of his own volition, this could be seen as another example of him scorning the family tradition and a further sign of his disdain.

Judah has three sons: Er, Onen, and Shelah (Gen. 38:3–5). This burst of successful fertility, in stark contrast to many other biblical characters, is an abundant blessing. Judah marries off his eldest son, Er, to an anonymous woman whose background and lineage are omitted from the text. All that is known about her is her name, Tamar, which is also the Hebrew word for "date" (Gen. 38:6). The date tree symbolizes the righteous (Ps. 92:13) and according to the Midrash, Tamar's comportment

2. Rashi on Genesis 38:2.
3. Rashi on that verse says Judah marries the daughter of a merchant, which is another reading of the word "Canaanite" based on Proverbs 31:24.

was as pleasing as the incense used in the Temple.[4] Her nationality is not mentioned, which leads one to surmise that she is not a Canaanite; if she was, surely that would be noted, as with the daughter of Shua. Er dies an unnatural death at the hand of God,[5] and Judah commands his next son, Onen, to marry his brother's widow as a form of levirate marriage (Gen. 38:8). Acting out of selfish concerns, Onen agrees to marry Tamar but refuses to impregnate her, and he too meets an untimely death.[6] Levirate marriage was practiced in ancient societies as a way of ensuring that the deceased's ancestral line would continue. A child born from such a union inherited his mother's first husband's property and maintained the first husband's name. Onen refuses to consider levirate marriage because any potential offspring from Tamar would not really be his own; they would belong to Er, his dead brother.

Interestingly, the previous chapter recounts Judah's insensitivity to his brother (by not using his influence to stop the sale of Joseph). Similarly, Judah's son Onen ignores his brother's legacy and honor. It appears that the message of responsibility to kin is attenuated in Judah's home. This argument is further supported by Judah leaving his brothers, betraying family traditions, and raising wayward sons.

The deaths of his two sons are a double tragedy for Judah. In the Bible, restitution for theft is to repay double the amount stolen. Perhaps this is God's way of exacting redress from Judah for the sale of Joseph. Having now experienced the trauma of losing children, it is puzzling that Judah doesn't return to his father and admit the truth regarding Joseph.

The deaths of two husbands must have been a crushing blow for Tamar, yet the text neglects to mention her suffering or even her reaction to the crises. Judah, suspecting that Tamar is the cause of their deaths and not willing to risk losing a third child, sends her back to her father's house, claiming that Shelah is too young to marry (Gen. 38:11). The implication is that he will allow her to marry Shelah when he is older,

4. *Midrash Lekaḥ Tov, Vayishlaḥ* 38:1:14.

5. See Genesis 38:7. In Hebrew, the name ער, "Er," read backward is רע, "evil."

6. Genesis 38:9–10. The verse says "he too," which the Sages explain to mean that Er's sin was the same as that of his brother. Er's rationale was that if Tamar did not become pregnant, she would retain her beauty.

though Judah has no such intention. Again, we see Judah behaving with considerable insensitivity. He puts Tamar in an impossible situation: She is engaged to Shelah and therefore not able to marry anyone else, but she is also blocked from marrying Shelah. Judah forces her into the position of lifelong widow, much like an *aguna*, a woman whose husband refuses to divorce her halachically, making it impossible for her to remarry.[7] An *aguna* can also be a woman who's husband is missing.

After abandoning his family and suffering the loss of two sons, Judah endures yet another tragedy when his wife dies prematurely (Gen. 38:12).

Encounter

We next see Judah heading out to participate in the sheep shearing ceremony. When Tamar is informed that he is traveling (Gen. 38:13), she decides to take advantage of the opportunity. It is unclear how exactly Tamar learns of Judah's whereabouts, but she must be keeping a close eye on Judah's household, as the things happening there are crucial to her future. Tamar is resigned to the fact that Judah will keep Shelah from ever marrying her (Gen. 38:14). It seems she must take control of her own destiny. With this in mind, she removes her widow's garb, covers her face with a veil, and waits for her father-in-law at the crossroads.

Judah mistakes Tamar for a common prostitute and propositions her, offering a goat kid as payment. He then avails himself of her services, leaving his signet ring, staff, and cloak as collateral for the payment that he promises to send. When Judah returns to exchange the goat for his security deposit, he cannot locate the "prostitute," not knowing that a pregnant Tamar has already returned to her father's house.

The text continues to describe Judah's surprising and destructive behavior pattern. Though prior to the giving of the Torah, prostitution was not prohibited,[8] and no infidelity has taken place as his wife has already died, Judah does not conduct himself according to the lofty moral standards that would be expected of a son of Jacob and the founding

7. Rashi on Genesis 38:11.
8. See Maimonides, *Sefer Nashim, Hilkhot Ishut* 1:4.

member of one of the tribes of God. The fact that Judah does not have any means of payment readily available indicates that it was an impulsive act, not a calculated, planned tryst, further unbefitting someone of Judah's background. The Midrash suggests that God put desire into his heart to help facilitate the conception of the Messiah.[9]

Tamar's intentions are less obvious. She has already buried two husbands and accepts that she will never marry Shelah. The classic commentators suggest two ways of understanding her actions. According to Rashi, she prepares a plan to seduce Judah (Gen. 38:14). She waits for him at the *petaḥ einayim*, literally, "opening of the eyes" of the crossroads, an unusual term that does not appear elsewhere in Tanakh. She waits by this road "that all eyes are turned to," the road to Hebron, the holy burial site of the forefathers and foremothers. Perhaps she hopes that her prayers in this particular spot will induce God to help her in Abraham's merit so that she can continue his family line.

With this approach, the remarkable audacity of her plan cannot be underscored enough, as there are innumerable possible pitfalls that could torpedo the scheme. What if she is not able to successfully entice Judah? The short-term nature of the rendezvous also makes the chance of conception quite remote; what will happen if she doesn't become pregnant? What if Judah (or someone else) recognizes her? What if he has the means of payment at his disposal, precluding her presentation of the identifying collateral when she is eventually called into question? This plan has a minimal chance of being successful; it could easily and catastrophically backfire.

Sforno argues that actually, Tamar plans to confront Judah at the crossroads without her mourning clothes (Gen. 38:14). She is hoping that Judah will then be reminded that he has neglected her, and allow her to marry Shelah after all. When he fails to identify her (as many years have gone by) and propositions her, she responds verbally, hoping that he will recognize her voice. When this also proves unsuccessful, she swiftly moves to plan B and agrees to Judah's proposition. Sforno contends that it was never her original plan to seduce him.

9. Genesis Rabba 85:1.

But this perspective is also fraught with difficulties. With this approach, the Torah would not need to mention Tamar's wardrobe change, as it would not serve a specific purpose. Also, if her intention is to arrange a meeting with her father-in-law, it would behoove her to send a male representative to intercede on her behalf. Her desperate state may be leading her to display dangerous and potentially harmful behavior.

According to Rashi, Judah does not recognize Tamar because her face was always modestly covered in his home when she was married to his son. Although she provocatively reveals her face at this fateful juncture, he doesn't recognize her.[10] Tamar now deceives Judah, just as he was less than honest with her.

Perhaps God prefers that Tamar's children come from Judah and not his sons, as they were born of a Canaanite woman. The Midrash claims that Tamar prays to God to not "let me leave the house empty,"[11] recognizing that her success is dependent upon God's intervention, reflecting her pure intentions.[12] It is interesting that Tamar's actions are not disapproved of in Jewish literature. To the contrary, in the book of Ruth, we find that Ruth is blessed to be like the house of Tamar and Judah (Ruth 4:11–12).

When Judah sends his messenger to retrieve his collateral, he is unable to find the prostitute, and the townspeople tell him that in fact, "no cult prostitute has been here" (Gen. 38:21). The Midrash[13] states that this represents divine affirmation of the legitimacy and pure intentions of Tamar's act. Indeed, Tamar has the great merit of giving birth to the great-great-grandfather of King David, and ultimately the Messiah.

Accused

Tamar returns to her father's home after the encounter, wearing her mourning clothes. Three months later, it becomes obvious that she is

10. Rashi on Genesis 38:14.
11. Genesis Rabba.
12. Rashi on Genesis 38:14.
13. *Midrash Sekhel Tov*, Genesis 38:22.

pregnant. When Judah hears of this, his initial reaction is to call for her death as an adulterer (Gen. 38:24).

Judah assumes the role of prosecutor, judge, and jury, condemning Tamar without due process. This is another example of his impulsiveness, much like the way he heartlessly condemns Joseph to a life of slavery without a fair trial.

As Tamar is brought out for execution, she presents Judah with the personal items that he gave her as a deposit, and she explains that the owner of these items is the father of her child.[14] Judah could have remained silent to avoid the guilt and shame, but faced with the unenviable choice of condemning an innocent woman to death or admitting his own guilt,[15] Judah finally distinguishes himself as a person of valor by admitting, *Tzadka mimeni*, "She is more righteous than I" (Gen. 38:26). He recognizes Tamar's fortitude in independently and rightfully expressing her grievance toward Judah for unjustly preventing her from marrying Shelah.

With this brief declaration, Judah recovers from his fallen state. In chapter 37, he sidestepped his responsibility toward Joseph – with tragic consequences. Now, in vivid contrast, Judah forthrightly confronts his misdeeds, admits his guilt, and saves Tamar's life.

True repentance is measured when the sinner experiences the same temptation but does not succumb to the sin again.[16] What qualifies Judah to be a suitable monarch is this ability to introspect and repent. Tamar has in her possession his signet ring, cloak, and staff, all symbols of kingship. All humans are flawed and fall prey to sin; the question is how one responds to such transgressions. Judah, with the help of Tamar, is able to transition from sinner to sovereign, reclaiming his monarchical items in the process.

---

14. She chooses not to name Judah so as not to embarrass him.
15. The Midrash (Exodus Rabba 30:19) claims that Abraham, Isaac, and all the brothers were present.
16. Maimonides, *Sefer HaMadda, Hilkhot Teshuva* 2:1.

The narrative continues[17] by pointing out that thereafter, Judah "did not know her."[18] Rashi quotes opposing opinions as to whether these words mean that Judah maintains his relationship with Tamar or they go separate ways. The explanation that Judah and Tamar do not remain intimately connected casts Judah in a more favorable light inasmuch as it would be morally repugnant to marry her after treating her as a prostitute, especially after having been responsible for her being led to the gallows.

Twins are born to Tamar and Judah, replacing his two deceased sons.

The analysis of the narrative started with the long view, with God silently directing from afar as the protagonists play their roles. What is exceedingly perplexing is the fact that Israel's grand redeemer, the one destined to usher in the Messianic Era of glorious spirituality, has a checkered history. Why does God, the ultimate playwright, author such a bizarre and bewildering script?

God's historical program requires a redeemer as part of the cast. He tailors the script to fit the human actions, behaviors, choices, and intentions surrounding which the Messiah's ancestors are created. This chapter closely parallels the previous chapter that describes the sale of Joseph and thereby reflects a clear punishment for Judah's indiscretions there. In both stories, Jacob and Judah are the subjects of a ruse, and the goat kid plays an integral part in both cases of deception. The brothers send Joseph's coat that has been dipped in blood and ask Jacob whether he recognizes it. Likewise, Tamar sends Judah his personal belongings and asks him whether he recognizes their owner.

Tamar's seduction of Judah is proven to be justified and even deemed righteous, worthy of resulting in the birth of the direct ancestor of the eventual Messiah. The Gaon of Brasov applies the lessons learned from the entire episode to modern Jewish history.[19] He suggests that

17. See Genesis 38:26. There is another opinion that Judah continues to have a relationship with Tamar.
18. Rashi offers two possibilities: Judah either never stops "knowing" her, or he never has relations with her again.
19. Rabbi David Sperber, *Michtam L'David, Parashat Vayeshev* (1944), 191.

although the founding fathers of the modern State of Israel may not have been beacons of religiosity, they boldly decided the time had come to remove the clothes of mourning and act. Perhaps their actions were questionable, but their motivations were pure. Just as Tamar conveys the message to Judah that the time has come to shed her mourner's attire and marry Shelah, the early Zionists were signaling to God that the time had come to cast off the cloak of exile and reconnect with our homeland.

Humanity does its part, and God, in a parallel world, does His.

Chapter 15

Ruth

There is a well-known joke that tells of a dangerous flood threatening a town. The police go door to door warning the town's inhabitants to evacuate. When they arrive at Jim's house, he refuses to leave, declaring, "No worries, I trust in God and He will save me!" The rain starts to fall; the tide rises and water begins to fill the streets. Fire rescue personnel come by in a boat and offer to take Jim to safety. He refuses, saying confidently, "I trust in God and He will save me!" The water continues to rise rapidly, and Jim climbs up to his roof. A helicopter flies by in a frantic, last-ditch effort to save him and deliver him to dry land. Expressing enormous faith, Jim politely but steadfastly declined the pleas of the rescue workers, announcing yet again, "I trust in God and He will save me!" The waters overcome him and he drowns, whereupon he appears before God in the heavenly court. Brazenly, he cries out, "God, why didn't You save me? I put all my trust in You!" God responds, "My dear Jim, who do you think sent the police, the fire department, and the helicopter?"

Life presents us with endless opportunities; the challenge is to recognize and take advantage of them. Often, when a chance is missed, no harm is done. At other times, however, we are forced to bear the consequences. The book of Ruth is about a number of characters, some who seize opportunities, some who miss their chance, and some who face unavoidable circumstances.

Beginning

To escape the famine in Israel, Elimelech, a wealthy community leader, leaves the Holy Land and settles in Moab. His affluent and distinguished family is accepted into the upper echelons of Moabite society. After assimilating into the local environment and culture, his two Jewish sons intermarry (Ruth 1:1–5). Elimelech and his sons reject their homeland, their nation, and eventually, God, all dying on foreign soil (Bava Batra 91b) as a result of the grave sin of abandoning their people.[1]

Elimelech is the leader of his generation, with sufficient means to support those around him. In leaving Israel, he withdraws his financial backing as well as his emotional support during this trying time. The Gemara speculates that he even ceases to pray for his kinfolk (Bava Batra 91a). His hasty departure in a time of crisis is undoubtedly a heavy and demoralizing blow to those he deserts, leaving them with feelings of abandonment and hopelessness.[2] He has no interest in helping the less fortunate,[3] and chooses to align himself with a nation that is historically renowned for its self-centered culture and lack of care for the downtrodden. For this reason, the Jewish nation, with our deep values and history of charity and loving-kindness, does not accept male Moabite converts. However, it appears that it is precisely this lack of a desire to help the needy that appeals to Elimelech and leads him to Moab. The ever-present responsibility of supporting those less fortunate is coldly neglected, and Elimelech and his sons die prematurely.

Naomi

Following the death of Elimelech and his sons, his widow Naomi emerges as the sole survivor of the once-prestigious family. She faces

1. Malbim on Ruth 1:3.
2. *Yalkut Shimoni* on Ruth, *remez* 598.
3. *Yalkut Shimoni* on Ruth, *remez* 560.

an unenviable choice: living sequestered in Moab with its foreign culture, or returning to her original, supportive home as a broken, childless widow. One can make the case that her punishment is even more severe than that of her husband and sons, as she bears the burdens of loneliness and destitution. Having left Israel as a wealthy dowager only to return as an abject, defeated woman to the very people whom her family rejected is not only difficult for Naomi, it is also uncomfortable for the community. They are now confronted with the awkward situation of a despondent woman who has nothing and is in need of encouragement, assistance, and pity, all while memories of her family's wealth, status, and abandonment of the community are undoubtedly fresh in their minds, tempering their enthusiasm to come to her aid.

Naomi chooses to ignore the humiliation and hardship, returning to the Land of Israel because "the Lord had brought His people to mind and granted them bread" (Ruth 1:6). God has returned to His nation by ending the famine; Naomi surmises that it is also time for her to return.

The word *shuv*, meaning "return," appears twelve times in the first chapter of Ruth. Naomi is returning: physically, to the land, and spiritually, to God. *Teshuva*, from the root S-U-V, signifying repentance, is a concept that God gifted to mankind, and every person has the ability to decide whether to seize the opportunity or not. This principle is a fundamental idea in Judaism, a pillar on which rests the totality of the Torah and mitzvot, as is stated in Deuteronomy 30:15: "See, I have set before you today life and goodness, and death and evil." Similarly, we find in Deuteronomy 11:26: "See this, I am setting before you on this day a blessing and a curse," implying that the choice is in our hands.[4]

Naomi does not squander the moment and chooses to return with her head bowed.

Daughters-in-Law

Naomi has two Moabite daughters-in-law, Orpah and Ruth.[5] These women remain with Naomi even after the deaths of their husbands and

4. Maimonides, *Sefer HaMadda, Hilkhot Teshuva* 5:3.
5. According to *Yalkut Shimoni* 600, the women never converted, though *Zohar Ḥadash*

express interest in joining her on the journey to Israel. While it would benefit Naomi for them to remain with her, as they could provide help and support, it would also be a public sign of the depth and magnitude of her family's shame.[6] Understanding the challenges ahead of her, Naomi encourages them to stay in Moab (Ruth 1:8). Initially, they refuse and cling to her (Ruth 1:9). She continues to urge them to stay in Moab, as she has little to offer them in the way of a future.

The two women are presented with the same opportunity. Orpah[7] chooses what is arguably the more reasonable path, heeding her mother-in-law's advice to return to her parents' home (Ruth 1:14). The difficulty of women in ancient times living without a male guardian is well known. With that in mind, her decision is objectively the intelligent, secure one.

While Orpah acts sensibly, Ruth's approach appears counterintuitive and illogical. She proclaims that she will not abandon Naomi as Orpah did, famously stating: "For wherever you walk, I shall walk, and wherever you stay, there I stay. Your people is my people; your God is my God" (Ruth 1:16–17). Ruth is willing to commit to God, undergo the conversion process, and adhere to His commandments. She expresses an unequivocal and unconditional love for Naomi, her nation, and her God.

No one knows what motivates these two individuals who share similar experiences to take divergent paths, but several generations later, the consequences of their momentous decisions become evident (Sota 42b). Orpah's descendant is the evil mammoth Goliath, who defames God. He is ultimately killed in battle by the righteous David, the descendant of Ruth. When people choose to take advantage of the opportunities presented to them by God, these decisions can have enormous ramifications for the future.

Townspeople

Naomi and her newly converted daughter-in-law Ruth return to Bethlehem (in Hebrew, *Beit Leḥem,* literally, "House of Bread"). They are

says they were converts.

6. Ruth Zuta 9.
7. According to Ruth Rabba 2, the name Orpah means "turn her back."

greeted with mocking disbelief: "Can this be Naomi?" (Ruth 1:19), as if to say, "Is this really the same person who left with everything and is now empty-handed?" Naomi, accepting the divine decree as part of her penance, explains that she has returned under difficult and painful circumstances.

The first chapter ends with Israel reaping the rewards of a bountiful barley harvest while Naomi and Ruth still suffer from the pangs of famine in Bethlehem. The people are presented with a marvelous opportunity to take pity on the downtrodden widow and her convert daughter-in-law and share God's gift of abundance with them, a core commandment that is repeated often in the Bible. Instead, the people appear to squander their chance to help. The text does not detail whether this is a calculated decision by the people – who are relatives of Naomi – to give the returnees the cold shoulder. One can speculate that they may be reacting negatively to the foreign-born Ruth. Alternatively, they may be too preoccupied with their own lives to see the needs of others.

Boaz

The narrative turns its focus toward Elimelech's nephew Boaz (Bava Batra 91a–92b). Although he is a wealthy landowner, he does not seize the opportunity to help his starving aunt.

As a poor person, Ruth has the biblical right to gather leftover grain from the edges of the fields.[8] Providentially, Ruth finds her way to the field of Boaz. When he determines her identity, he allows her to continue gleaning safely. Although he is upholding the mitzva of *pe'ah*, gleaning, this is in fact a missed opportunity and a failure on Boaz's part. He is now clearly aware of Naomi and Ruth's poverty. What he offers is mandated by the Bible – but he could have done more. He could have told Naomi to go home and arrange for a food parcel to be delivered every morning to her door. Instead, she continues gleaning from his field for three months, throughout the harvest season.[9]

8. See Leviticus 19:9–10.
9. *Yalkut Shimoni* 604.

An Opportunity You Can't Turn Down

With the end of the harvest season, Naomi and Ruth are again faced with hunger. Naomi devises a plan to present Boaz with an opportunity he can't ignore. It is the plan of a desperate woman. She asks Ruth to go down to the threshing floor and seduce Boaz, forcing him to redeem the family by fulfilling the mitzva of *yibum*, levirate marriage (Ruth 3:3–4). Naomi does not suggest redeeming the family in this way through a matchmaker because she does not want to give him the option of refusal.

In the middle of the night, after preparing herself with a dress and perfume, Ruth finds Boaz asleep on the threshing floor and lies down at his feet. Fear overtakes Boaz when he discovers a woman at his side. Ruth identifies herself and her purpose: "I am your maidservant Ruth – spread your mantle over your maidservant, for you are a redeemer" (Ruth 3:9).

This time, Boaz recognizes his responsibility to his aunt and deceased cousins and promises Ruth that he will deal with the situation. Boaz explains that there is a relative who has priority in the order of performing *yibum* (Ruth 3:12). He swears that first thing in the morning, he will clarify who should take responsibility for redeeming her.

Ploni Almoni

Indeed, Boaz goes out in the morning and finds the "redeemer." Boaz gives this unidentified relative the opportunity to redeem the field of Elimelech, which he agrees to. Boaz then adds that along with the field comes Ruth, who needs to be married to "restore the dead man's name on his estate" (Ruth 4:5). The relative turns down this opportunity, thereby losing the chance to become the grandfather of the Messiah. This man is not punished for not taking the opportunity God sends him – he has not committed a sin – but he becomes nothing more than a footnote in history. He is referred to as Ploni Almoni, the equivalent of a John Doe, a nobody.

Conclusion

Boaz redeems the field and marries Ruth. The women who had previously ostracized Naomi celebrate with her, acknowledging Ruth and recognizing the blessing she has brought. Ruth and Boaz have a son, whom they name Oved. In time, he becomes the grandfather of King David and the forefather of the Messiah.

The Book of Ruth reveals to the reader what happens to those who take advantage of the opportunities that God presents, as well as what happens to those who pass them up. The first person in this book to miss an opportunity is Elimelech. As the *gadol hador* and a person of significant wealth, he could have helped the people of his town but instead chose to run and ends up dead, buried in a foreign land with his children intermarried to the local women.

When Naomi hears that God has remembered His people, she chooses to return. One daughter-in-law is perceptive enough to see the opportunity; she goes with Naomi and becomes the grandmother of the Messiah. The other turns her back and becomes the grandmother of the evil giant Goliath. Upon returning to Bethlehem, the closest relative is given an opportunity to marry and redeem Ruth, but he is afraid, and as a result, he literally becomes an anonymous personality, a nobody. Boaz, who himself does not initially rise to the occasion, eventually does take the opportunity presented to him – he redeems Ruth and becomes the forefather of the Messiah.

COMPARISON BETWEEN THE THREE STORIES

There are three stories that play a role in the birth of King David and his descendant, the Messiah. Although they are separate stories, they contain a number of important similarities. It is the major difference in the Ruth version that "fixes" (i.e., spiritually repairs) the mistakes of the earlier biblical personalities.

Daughters of Lot	Tamar (daughter-in-law of Judah)	Ruth
Separation from brothers	Separation from brothers	Separation from brothers
Immoral culture: Sodom	Immoral culture: Canaan	Immoral culture: Moab
Two daughters without husbands	Two dead sons	Two dead sons
Destroyed family/ abandoned	Destroyed family/ abandoned	Destroyed family/ abandoned
Unusual location: cave	Unusual location: on the road	Unusual location: silo
Older woman is proactive	Woman is proactive	Older woman is proactive
Good intentions	Good intentions	Good intentions
Yibum (levirate marriage)	*Yibum* (levirate marriage)	*Yibum* (levirate marriage)
Trickery	Trickery	No trickery
Lot doesn't know what happened	Judah doesn't recognize Tamar	Boaz clarifies who Ruth is
Incest	Incest	No incest
Childless	Childless	Childless
Immediate pregnancy	Immediate pregnancy	Immediate pregnancy
Wandering	Wandering	Wandering
God's involvement	God's involvement	God's involvement
Two sons born	Two sons born	Son born
Misguided *ḥesed*	Inadequate responsibility	Rectified

A comparison of these three stories, which serve as the backdrop to the birth of the Messiah, reveals many commonalities. However, though the similarities are striking, the differences are even more significant. In the stories of the daughters of Lot and Tamar, we find elements of dishonesty and trickery, in which a woman takes advantage of an unsuspecting man, but in the Ruth story, when Boaz asks Ruth to identify herself, she does so honestly and without hesitation. In this way, Ruth takes the good intentions and kindness of the earlier characters, and rectifies their problematic behavior. The daughters of Lot try to save the world – a kindness of great proportions – but their method is questionable. Ruth, who personifies *ḥesed,* tells the truth even when she is placed in a questionable position at the behest of her mother-in-law, and in doing so, she rectifies the sin of the daughters of Lot.

Boaz, like his forefather Judah, initially does not take responsibility for his relatives. But when Ruth comes to him in the silo, he rises to the occasion. He does not have relations with her that night (which would have been like sleeping with another man's wife, as she is designated to be married off to the closest relative). Rather, he understands the importance of his responsibility, and he ensures that justice is done for Ruth. In this way, he brings about *tikkun olam,* "fixing" the world spiritually by repairing Judah's avoidance of responsibility.

Chapter 16

Jerusalem

The New Colossus
Not like the brazen giant of Greek fame,
with conquering limbs astride from land to land;
here at our sea-washed, sunset gates shall stand
a mighty woman with a torch, whose flame
is the imprisoned lightning, and her name
Mother of Exiles...

Emma Lazarus, 1883

The iconic Statue of Liberty, emblazoned with this poem by Emma Lazarus, has become the symbol of the welcoming female character who majestically greets downtrodden refugees. She holds the torch whose flame serves as a beacon for all those seeking redemption.

As a Barren Woman

Jerusalem is likewise described as a female whose glowing light illuminates the entire world.[1]

The *Naḥem* prayer recited on Tisha BeAv, the fast of the ninth of Av, includes the dramatic anthropomorphic depiction of the bereft holy city: "She [Jerusalem] sits [in her house] with her head covered, like

1. *Pesikta DeRav Kahana* 21:4.

a barren woman who has not borne." After the destruction, a forlorn Jerusalem painfully recalls her children who have been violently torn from her embrace. She is barren; without her inhabitants there is little hope of continuity, both literally and figuratively. Interestingly, since the reunification of Jerusalem in 1967, there has been some discussion about modifying the wording of this prayer to reflect a less mournful tone.

Isaiah 54:1, one of the *haftarot* of consolation, begins: "Barren woman, never a mother, rejoice." Jerusalem is likened to a desperate barren woman who sees no hope for a future, but is promised by the prophet that eventually, a multitude of children will fill her tents. The barren woman is a metaphor for desolation, the inability to produce, nurture, develop, or grow. It reflects the despair and hopelessness of the Diaspora. Although a childless couple suffers daily, the knowledge that their future is bleak exacerbates their anguish even more. There is no one to care for them in their old age, perpetuate their name, keep their memory alive, or say *Kaddish* for them. Just as barrenness is seen as an anomalous predicament, so too is it anomalous for a Jew to live in the Diaspora. The seeming endlessness of the exile, regardless of whether it is benevolent or harsh, is discouraging and makes the future uncertain and, at times, frightening.

As the barren woman eventually gives birth, so too will Jerusalem ultimately be redeemed. The prophet consoles and assures the Jewish people that the nation will be rebuilt with expanded borders, prosperity, and revived cities.[2] Earlier complications and obstacles will be eliminated and Israel's special relationship with God will be renewed. Jerusalem will be filled with splendor and justice, never to be destroyed again as her inhabitants enjoy peace and tranquility. They will be respected and emulated by the nations of the world, thereby bringing honor to God.

Salvation

Isaiah portrays Jerusalem as four different types of women, all of whom need to be rescued from their grave predicaments. Jerusalem is described

2. It is for this reason that in addition to reading this chapter of Isaiah as the *haftara* for *Parashat Noaḥ*, it is read during the seven weeks of consolation after Tisha BeAv.

as barren (54:1), widowed (54:4–5), abandoned (54:6–7), and poor (54:11). Jerusalem will be rescued from these difficult circumstances with the ingathering of the exiles and the rebuilding of the city, ushering in an era of wealth, peace, and serenity.

The word in Hebrew for barren, *akara*, means "uproot."[3] Jerusalem is an *akara* because her children have been uprooted from her borders and relocated to foreign lands, leaving her childless. Rachel is also referred to as an *akara* (Gen. 29:31); the Midrash relates the term to her standing as the primary wife (the *ikar*).[4] In the Book of Ruth, when the wedding guests bless her, they say: "May the Lord bestow upon the woman who comes into this house [as was bestowed upon] Rachel and Leah who have built the House of Israel" (4:11.) Rachel's name precedes her older sister's, indicating that she is held in higher esteem. Rachel's influence is so strong that although she is the biological mother of only two tribes, she is associated with the entire nation. Jeremiah describes Rachel's wailing in Ramah for her lost children and her refusal to be comforted, as her sons have been banished from their home (Jer. 31:14). The fact that she is buried alone on the road to Bethlehem, separated from the rest of the forefathers and foremothers in Hebron, is also an exile of sorts, although this location allows her descendants to implore her to beseech God on their behalf. When she subsequently tearfully turns to God, He answers her, as opposed to all the other forefathers: "Cease your crying. There is a reward for your actions. Your sons will return to their land."[5]

Isaiah comforts Jerusalem by telling of the return of not only some of her children, but many future offspring – and not only will they return, but there will also be architectural growth and expansion. This eases the daily pain that Jerusalem is now experiencing. She realizes that the feeling is temporary, that a future bright with hope and promise beckons. Just as the foremothers were unable to conceive yet ultimately, they were miraculously blessed with children, Jerusalem is destined to be miraculously restored with the redeemed exiles returning

3. *Pesikta DeRav Kahana* 20.
4. Genesis Rabba 71:2.
5. *Pesikta Eikha Rabba* 24.

to her midst: "Break out in joyful song though you have not given birth" (Isaiah 54:1). And earlier, the prophet tells us: Zion will say, "Who bore these children?" (49:21).

Creation

The Midrash lists seven biblical women who suffered from infertility.[6] Unexpectedly, Zion is also included. These seven women parallel the seven days of Creation:

1. First is Sarah, as it is written, "And Sarai was barren" (Gen. 11:30). She is parallel to the first day, and what was created on the first day? Heaven and earth. Her husband gave possession of these to the Holy One, as it says, "Blessed be Avram by God Most High, Maker of heaven and earth" (Gen. 14:19).
2. The second is Rebecca, as it says, "And Isaac pleaded with the Lord on behalf of his wife for she was childless" (Gen. 25:21). She is parallel to day two, and what was created on day two? The firmament: "So God made the expanse, and it separated the water beneath the expanse from the water above" (Gen. 1:7). So too Rebecca gave birth to two – Jacob and Esau, as it says: "I have set you apart from all other peoples" (Lev. 20:26).
3. The third is Leah, as it says: "And when the Lord saw that Leah was unloved, He opened her womb" (Gen. 29:31). She is parallel to day three, of which it is written: "Let the earth produce vegetation" (Gen. 1:11). Reuben was Leah's son, as it says: "During the wheat harvest, Reuben went for a walk" (Gen. 30:14).
4. The fourth is Rachel, parallel to day four. What was created then? The sun, the moon, the stars and the constellations, as it says: "And God said, 'Let there be lights'" (Gen. 1:14). Joseph, Rachel's son, stood up while his brothers bowed to him, as it says: "The sun, the moon, and eleven stars were bowing down to me" (Gen. 37:9).
5. The fifth is Hannah, parallel to day five. What was created on day five? "Let birds fly over the earth" (Gen. 1:20). So too Hannah's son

6. Genesis Rabba 53:3. There is a similar midrash in *Pesikta DeRav Kahana* 20:1.

Shmuel was like a bird, flitting from place to place, from country to country and in the end returning to his nest. And so too, Shmuel was occupied with the business of Israel, going to every place, as it says: "Year after year, he would make his rounds... before returning to Ramah, for there was his home" (I Sam. 7:16–17).

6. The sixth is Hazlelponi, the mother of Samson, as it says: "And their sister's name was Hazlelponi" (I Chr. 4:3). She is parallel to day six, and what was created on day six? Man. And what happened to man? He died at the hand of his wife, as it says: "And to man He said, 'Because you listened to your wife'" (Gen. 3:17). Samson her son also died at the hands of his wife, as it says: "He fell in love with a woman from Sorek Stream, whose name was Delilah" (Judges 16:4). "And the Philistines seized him, and gouged out his eyes" (Judges 16:21).
7. The seventh is Zion, and what is written regarding it? "And He rested on the seventh day" (Ex. 20:11). And about Zion: "This is My resting place for all time" (Ps. 132:14). Therefore, Isaiah said: "Break out in joyful song though you have not given birth" (Is. 54:1).

The only way to comprehend and appreciate Israel's national suffering is by comparing it to the agony that these exceptional women endured. The Midrash likens each woman to a day of Creation. Zion corresponds to the seventh day, Shabbat, the holiest and most exclusive. The Creation narrative, which details the genesis of the universe, is used as a foil for women who long to create children but lack the capacity to do so.

Return

These women, who were responsible for laying Judaism's spiritual foundation, ultimately have their yearnings satisfied, as Zion's cravings will be fulfilled when her exiled children return home. On Rosh HaShana, the day of the world's conception, we read Jeremiah's prophecy about the salvation of Zion's exiled children and their return to their homeland.[7] The birthing mother who breathes new life into her newborn is equated with Zion, which at the time of the final redemption suffuses

7. Jeremiah 31 is the *haftara* reading for the second day of Rosh HaShana.

an embattled, beleaguered, and barely recognizable Israel with a fresh, new spirit.

Psalms 113:9 praises God as "He settles the childless woman in her home as a joyous mother of children." The Midrash describes childless women as pitiful captives who remain ensconced in their homes, the joy and fulfillment of motherhood eluding them. Then, when God eventually remembers them, they stand tall.[8] In ancient times, when bearing children was considered a woman's *raison d'être,* infertile women would prefer to remain within the protective walls of their homes in order to avoid openly displaying their shame and ignominy to their friends and neighbors. When God cedes to their pleas and grants them children, they also remain in the home, but now as satisfied and jubilant mothers feeling blessed and privileged to engage in the loving task of child-rearing. While this chapter describes the salvation that God brings to society's most underserved, the poor and the destitute, the salvation granted to the barren woman exceeds even the allotment that God accords to those unfortunate souls.

Ascribing to Zion, an inanimate entity, the mortal characteristics associated with Judaism's forefathers and foremothers underscores this powerful connection. It is a relationship that has no corollary in the world. The underlying message of comparing Zion to the nation's matriarchs is that both represent the source and the home. Just like a child comes from his mother, a Jew should view himself as coming from Zion. Both Zion and the matriarchs are responsible for birth and development; both delight in their children's achievements and are tormented by their shortcomings. They instruct their offspring as to what warrants their concern and attention and what values are worth fighting for. They imbibe their souls with tradition, security, and faith. Their reciprocal love is deep and abiding and their fates and destinies are intertwined.

---

8. Genesis Rabba 71:1–2.

God's Love

The Gemara (Berakhot 10a) discusses a meeting between a heretic and Beruria, the famous wife of R. Meir and the daughter of R. Ḥanina:

An apostate said to Beruria: "It is written, 'Break out in joyful song though you have not given birth' (Is. 54:1). Is the woman to sing because she did not bear children?" She answered him, "Fool, glance at the end of the verse, for it is written, 'For the children of the forsaken woman will outnumber those of the wife.' But what does it mean when it says, 'Barren woman, never a mother'? Sing, O community of Israel, who is like a barren woman who has not borne children for Gehinom, like you."

Beruria lost two children in her lifetime; hers is a different kind of barrenness. When her esteemed husband became distraught upon hearing the tragic news, she reminded him of God's plan and gift (Berakhot 10a). The heretic challenges her faith in light of her loss. Basing her response on this verse, she rebukes the heretic and argues that at times there might be some value to childlessness. She rationalizes that it is preferable to die rather than live as sinners like the heretic's children. Exile, punishment, and loss are equivalent to infertility. At times, suffering is necessary, a part of God's agenda, and in the long view of history, that will eventually become clear.

In a paean of God's love for Israel, Isaiah prophesies that the emancipated nation will return from the Diaspora in numbers greater than those who lived in Jerusalem prior to the exile. At the time of their return, joy and happiness will supplant solitude and suffering (Is. 54:1–17). Jerusalem will need to expand her city limits to accommodate the population growth (54:2–3). The experience will be so glorious that the miseries and adversities that the Jewish people endured while progressing through their grueling history will be forgotten. Israel is reassured that God, as their Creator and master, still maintains His special relationship with His nation and will vanquish their enemies.

God, the beloved husband, who may seem to have disappeared and is assumed by many to be dead, will return to reestablish the love of His youth. The female Jerusalem will no longer be widowed or childless. In the Messianic Era, the days of exile and punishment will seem fleeting when compared to the lengthy redemption. The renewal of the everlasting covenant will be stronger than even the forces of nature. Jerusalem, impoverished, alone, and desolate will be comforted by God as He envelopes her in a blanket of precious jewels.[9] All Jerusalem's inhabitants will be learned, and they will live with an abundance of peace. No physical or spiritual destruction will again harm Jerusalem, as all will recognize that the truth is with her. Metaphorically, in a brief moment, the enemy, Babylonia, will be transformed from the smug and entitled woman into a helpless widow who mourns her deceased children in an unexpected twist of fate (Is. 47:8–9).

Supernatural

The comparison between a barren woman and Jerusalem is instructive. Just as the experience of a woman who has no ability to conceive and carry to term yet manages to bear children defies the basic laws of nature and can be viewed as "supernatural," so the dispersed and downtrodden Jewish people's repopulation of their ancient, barren city can also be viewed as miraculous. The flourishing and rebuilding of an infertile, rocky land after years of desolation is an outgrowth of that miracle. The nation of Israel, the city of Jerusalem, and the State of Israel are gifts from God that serve a special purpose and whose existence is so improbable that they can be considered as existing beyond the natural order. In contemporary times, Jerusalem's children have returned to her ever-expanding borders. Just over one hundred years ago, Mark Twain described Jerusalem as a pathetic, neglected city that could be traversed in a day,[10] a feat that would be impossible today. It is incontrovertible that many of Isaiah's messianic prophecies have occurred with the establishment of the modern State of Israel. Jews the world over hope and pray that the strides that have been made in recent generations truly represent the dawn of the Messianic Era and a period of history in which the word of God will be disseminated throughout humanity.

9. See Isaiah 54:12. The Hebrew word for "stone" (אבן) hints at the son (בן), the foundation of the family's continuation. See also Berakhot 64a.
10. Mark Twain, *The Innocents Abroad*, chapter 56 (London: 1881).

One of the traditional blessings recited at a marriage ceremony is: "Bring intense joy and exultation to the barren one through the ingathering of her children amidst her in gladness. Blessed are You, God, who gladdens Zion through her children."

May we live in a time that the words of this long-anticipated blessing are fulfilled!

Anne's Story: City of Prophecy

By Anne Gordon

In 2005, I came back to Jerusalem, having lived there in the nineties, and found that many of my landmarks in neighborhoods beyond the one that had been my own were gone. They'd been built up and around and over. A friend drove me through all the areas with spanking, brand-new buildings so I could get my bearings, but I couldn't. I asked her, "Where's thus-and-such building?" It was a large facility, and I knew I'd be able to identify it by the large empty wasteland of a field across the street, the one with a stark metal stick and a small sign indicating the bus stop. She said, "It's right there!"

The wasteland of a field had been replaced by classy, four-story Jerusalem stone apartment buildings. They looked lovely. Appealing. But the expansion of the city beyond the outskirts I'd known startled me.

I never encountered the barren, withered Jerusalem outside of the texts that provide Jewish history; the foundation of the modern Jewish state precedes my birth by more than twenty years. For me, Jerusalem has always been a bouncy, noisy, jumbled, hectic place of business ... and daily life ... and religious sounds and moves, punctuated by pockets of serenity. Lookouts with a view of the Old City or the Judean Hills, with a sky that seems touchable, clouds waiting to be plucked out of the blue (I'm told it's a trick of the land's placement to the east of the sea, but it seems intentional, a nearly tangible reminder of the Divine who is there for us all). The city's mix of ancient with the newest of new is intensity embodied, whether by dint of spirituality or personality, with frustration and passion running hand in hand, from the muezzin to car horns to babies caterwauling to the nonstop drilling that renews the modern city. We know the history, to be sure, but the idea that Jerusalem was once desolate is laughable – nearly as laughable as the foxes that once confirmed its desolation (Makkot 24).

The Jerusalem I know is vibrant. It is a city of yearning, yes, but not because of the promise of a reborn city. The city has already been reborn, the site of dreams sparked and embraced and fulfilled. The Jerusalem stone plays host to those who brought their wishes to the heart of a land, a people, a city surrounded by hills. They come to live their lives, to settle down for the duration, and they come because of the eternal holiness that helps them figure out what they want out of life, a way to balance priorities and shed light on what matters most.

I was living in Jerusalem when a friend suggested I freeze my eggs. I was past forty, and Mr. Right was not banging down my door (despite some promising false starts, and even a broken engagement). We all know the math (and the science): I could find the right guy later (I hoped), but I wouldn't be able to bear my own children forever. Freezing my eggs wasn't really where I was at, I realized. The question was whether I wanted to try for a family on my own.

First, I needed to determine whether I was even eligible to do so.

Three years later, after a zillion blood tests, doctors' exams, hormone shots, and ultrasounds, plus five IUIs, three IVFs, and something like seventy-two hours of labor, a curious, loving baby boy with his own fierce intensity and ultimate sweetness – someone told me he has an old soul – answered that question, and so many more.

It is no accident that it was in Jerusalem that I recognized that I could try for a family on my own. After all, this was the place to which I had returned as an *ola*, an immigrant, one of the many who – simply by making *aliya* – are bringing the Jewish people home from thousands of years of exile.

The money was part of it; I can't ignore that. Financial support from Israel's socialized medicine was essential. But it was more than that. Jewish identity is tangible in Jerusalem – as part of a person's sense of self, yes, but also as a member of the tribe, or better yet, the family. The woman on line at the post office who worried that my infant needed a hat (he was very warm already, thank you), the elderly couple who helped me load my groceries onto the supermarket's too-short conveyor belt when I was navigating purchases and trying to fend off the beginning of a meltdown, the woman at the tax authority who gave the toddler paper and pen to draw while we discussed complications of my freelance work – these encounters with strangers stayed with me not only because they were caring, but because they made it clear that we were all essentially and fundamentally connected. They helped out because of course they did. And in so doing, they upheld the blessing of my family.

For Jerusalem is a city that welcomes families of all shapes and sizes – from the hasidic woman who is mother to seventeen to the default Israeli nuclear families of two parents and four children, and my own tiny family of two. From the couples who aren't couples at all, but co-parents, using reproductive technologies for the sake of parenthood, even though they're never going to live under one roof – to the man and woman I know who began that way, and then unexpectedly married each other, already co-parents of two. Indeed, Jerusalem prioritizes children. An example: Each fall, first graders are welcomed to their school careers with the type of hoopla and fanfare the Western world associates with graduation. "*Shalom, kita alef!* – Welcome, first graders!" sparks eager anticipation and even joy. Just ask my boy, who grins from ear to ear at the sight of the little 'uns beginning school, though he left first grade behind some years ago.

Sabras have been known to ask those of us immigrants who arrived here by choice, not fleeing persecution, what brought us here, to this hot, dusty, conflict-bound, security-risk, expensive state that is modern Israel. Whyever would we want to scrabble to eke out our existence here, when we could live higher on the hog in our countries of origin? Most people I know acknowledge the economic challenges (especially if you start talking real estate), but for so many, the sense of coming home, the instinctive belonging in the place that we, the Jewish people, were promised to inherit, the roots of thousands of years of heritage, along with the ingathering of diverse exiles – the family that we were always a part of, but often distant from, in the Diaspora – triumph in the face of those difficulties.

The prophet Zechariah foretells the return of God to Zion, His dwelling place, to Jerusalem, the "city of truth," and the return of the very elderly to the city's squares (8:3–4). Those who are so old that they need staff in hand to support themselves are presented as the representatives of peace. They are R. Akiva's reassurance that the city will truly be rebuilt. They can't go out to do battle, so if they're able to hang out in the square, things around them must be pretty good. And according to Zechariah, those squares (dare I call them "playgrounds"?) are to be filled with boys and girls. These are the families of Jerusalem – the multiple generations that belong to everyone – those who have gone before and those who are to follow after. It's the birthday parties we hold in the parks, the parades that march through Jerusalem streets for special occasions, the chatter and yelling and laughter and music of family life shed from one apartment to the next, and the help with bundles and directions and advice to one and all, even to the people one doesn't like very much. Jerusalem thus offers the past and the future to the Jewish people. As a vibrant city, in this day and age, Jerusalem depends on the strength of each future generation to keep her going, just as that same vibrancy, with its roots in antiquity, its reach in modernity, and its growth by the will of God is the backbone that keeps me, my family, and the Jewish people going, surrounded by the echoes of prophecy.

Rabbanit Anne Gordon is the deputy editor of *Ops & Blogs* at *The Times of Israel.* A veteran educator living in Jerusalem, she co-hosts both the daily podcast *Talking Talmud* and *The Chochmat Nashim Podcast.* Her forthcoming book, part of Sefaria's Word-by-Word fellowship, is a study of Proverbs in rabbinic literature.

Conclusion

The Midrash explains that there are seven barren women.[1] The first six are Sarah, Rebecca, Rachel, and Leah, the mother of Samson, and Hannah. The midrash starts us off on our journey of exploring the connection of women to their desire to have children. The seventh "woman" on the list is the city of Jerusalem. Maybe it is only through the connection to real, individual experiences of infertility that we can understand this pain on a national level.

In addition, the midrash begins with the history of the Jewish people – who from the start are in need of miraculous, divine intervention – and takes us through until the end of time when, hopefully soon, Jerusalem will miraculously become fertile and filled with life. Jewish history is one long, continuous struggle for existence and continuity, which are dependent on the grace of God.

Unsurprisingly, the story of the birth of the nation of Israel includes birth metaphors.[2] The Jews go through a period of gestation, in which they exist within the "womb" of another nation, the Egyptians. There they experience darkness, yet they grow and develop. Then,

1. *Pesikta DeRav Kahana* 20.
2. Orit Avnery, "Pesach Is Literally the Story of a People's Birth," available at: https://www.hartman.org.il/pesach-is-literally-the-story-of-a-peoples-birth/.

through the plagues, they are born, breaking through the waters of the Sea of Reeds, emerging on the other side as a newborn nation.

Alternatively, one can view the forty years that the Jews spend in the desert as a parallel to the forty weeks of pregnancy. All the Israelites' needs are taken care of in the desert, from food to temperature. They don't even produce any waste, just like a fetus in its mother's womb. Traditionally, the role of the mother is to provide food and water to her children, just as God provides for the Israelites in the desert.

Although the stories that we have studied seem to be specific to the individual personalities, the ultimate message is that each of these stories has significance and relevance to our national challenges. From the barren mothers, we learn different ways of dealing with adversity, and we learn about the roles women can play as parents and influencers. Hazlelponi teaches that women have superior insight, the ability to see and understand events in a way that is different from men. Hannah teaches about the necessity of partnering with God, and from the Shunamite woman, we see the importance of appreciating what we have and acknowledging that everything in life, good and bad, originates from God – and that we have a responsibility to give back in some way.

In these stories, men make poor decisions that have a negative impact on the women in their lives. We see David's daughter Tamar and the daughter of Jephthah, victims whose lives are ruined. Michal, too, is but a pawn in the world of men and does not live happily ever after. On the other hand, Batya is able to manipulate the patriarchal world around her for her benefit, raising a child as her own.

A woman's natural tendency is to harbor and protect her children, alive or dead. The wife of Obadiah shows the determination of a mother to protect her children. Similarly, the prostitute who seeks help from Solomon is willing to give away her child in order to save his life, and Rizpah sacrifices herself to ensure that her dead children are given respect and dignity.

Athaliah becomes the mother who is too selfish to be able to give to others and has no compunctions, emotions, or moral compass. She is unfit to be a mother.

The daughters of Lot, although their means are questionable, do achieve a positive end. Judah's daughter-in-law Tamar takes control of her situation, achieves her goals, and enables Judah to repair and repent. She is the facilitator of his – and thereby the world's – repentance and redemption. Ruth, in fixing the questionable deeds of the daughters of Lot, takes advantage of the opportunities presented to her and becomes the grandmother of the Messiah.

Through studying these biblical personalities, we learn that the story of the nation of Israel is indeed as miraculous as the stories of the barren women who become mothers. We appreciate the strength and fortitude that these biblical women exhibit in order to birth, maintain, and educate future generations.

At first glance, we may have assumed that the themes of womanhood, fertility, birth, and child-rearing are not central to our national story. It is time to rethink this conclusion.

The fonts used in this book are from the Arno family

Maggid Books
The best of contemporary Jewish thought from
Koren Publishers Jerusalem Ltd.